Help!
I'm a Deacon's Wife

D1125628

Help!
I'm a Deacon's Wife

CONVENTION PRESS
Nashville, Tennessee

Contents

Introduction

Robert Sheffield

As it became widely known we would produce a book for deacons' wives, several questions surfaced. One of these involved the need for such a book. That answer came easily. For some time deacons' wives attending various conferences that we led have asked us when we would publish a book for them. The previous book by Martha Nelson has been in print for a number of years, and the feeling among many was that a new book was needed. I received this feeling most strongly from the ladies who lead conferences for deacons' wives. This book, then, comes as a result of an overwhelming request from wives and conference leaders in the churches of the Southern Baptist Convention.

Another question concerned the contents of the book. What topics needed to be addressed in a book of this nature? Since I am not a deacon's wife, I enlisted the help of some deacons' wives from around the country to write the book. The topics covered in this book are a result of conversations I had with these ladies. Of course, not all of the suggested topics could be included. We have included those topics that were identified most often. The content topics also were chosen because of their practical application to the role in which deacons' wives find themselves.

The other important question which required an answer before the book could be written involved who would write the various chapters. I would not write the book. Since I am not a deacon's wife, I could not understand all the dynamics involved in serving in this strategic role. In selecting those who would write the book, we turned to ladies who had experience in writing and/or leading conferences. All of them share the reality of living a ministering life-style as a deacon's wife. They know from personal experience what it means to serve in many roles at one time. These writers bring practical experience and helpful suggestions to their particular subjects.

To illustrate this I offer a summary from each chapter.

Chapter 1.—In this chapter Barbara Sheffield explores the role of the deacon, the role of the deacon's wife, and the roles they share. We are reminded that the deacon serves as a minister in the life of the church. In so doing, the deacon acts as a servant of the Lord to the church. Deacon responsibilities involve the task areas of leadership, proclamation, and caregiving.

The role of a deacon's wife can best be summed up in supporting her husband as he ministers and ministering alongside him. This chapter also gives some practical suggestions on how a deacon's wife can accomplish these responsibilities.

Finally, this chapter points out that the deacon and his wife need to share in ministry by growing spiritually; witnessing together; making ministering visits together; and being faithful, active, and peacemaking members of their local church. They need to be a strong example of Christian family life.

Chapter 2.—This chapter will help you, as a deacon's wife, handle the time pressures of your many roles. The author, Faye Robbins, accomplishes this through a series of personal lessons she learned concerning how to thrive and not just survive. These lessons include something she learned in the kitchen, from daylight savings time, from a college roommate, at PraiSing II, in learning to play the piano, from observing a busy person, while on a mountain, from a jonquil, while praying, and during a bout with cancer.

Chapter 3.—Fayly Cothern gives guidance in "Continuing to Grow." She indicates the way to continue growing involves committing the you God called, remembering your covenant with God, focusing on the Father, spending time with God, sharing in fellowship with other Christians, ministering in your giftedness, and maintaining a teachable mode.

Chapter 4.—Denise George provides helpful hints on how to balance all of the roles in which a busy deacon's wife, like yourself, serves. She gives guidance on how to handle the everyday stresses of life. She writes about the art of communication in the home. She gives suggestions on how to keep the romance alive in your marriage and how to keep your marriage strong. She also includes a helpful section on what to do to disagree properly with your spouse.

Chapter 5.—Barbara Sheffield details some practical ways in which you can minister as a deacon's wife. She does this by emphasizing the uniquenesses that each person brings to a ministry situation. She writes about finding easier ways to accomplish tasks, learning to delegate, earning the right to minister to some people, and being involved in follow-up ministries. In the appendix she has included some "easy to put together" recipes. Try some of these recipes as you minister to others through your kitchen.

The final section of the book is a list of recommended resources. Information in these resources will help you understand more about the role of deacon and help you minister more effectively.

I am glad you chose to read this book. I think you can tell from the chapter summaries that you will be glad you did. When you have finished reading the book, tell others about the blessing you received so they can read it also. Better yet, why not give the book as a gift?

I would also suggest the deacons' wives in your church study this book. In a group setting, each person can share experiences and learn from the experiences of others. This is especially helpful to the wives of newly ordained deacons. However you make use of the book, I commend you on your interest in being better equipped to serve in your role as the wife of a deacon.

Robert Sheffield is national consultant in deacon ministry, LifeWay Christian Resources, Nashville, Tennessee.

Chapter 1

Serving Together

Barbara Sheffield

His Role

Shannon sat listening to Harold, the deacon nominating committee chairperson, talk to her husband, Zachary, about becoming a deacon. Questions flooded her mind. Yes, she wanted to know what Zachary's role was going to be. How would his decision to become a deacon change their lives? What would be her role? What would the church expect from Zachary? from her?

When she had the opportunity, Shannon asked Harold to help her answer some of her questions.

The Bible shapes our understanding.—Harold began by explaining the meaning of the word *deacon*. The word *deacon* (*diakonos* in the Greek language) means servant or minister. This word was not given to deacons in the beginning. In its first usage the word applied to the whole church. Each Christian receives the charge to minister as a servant of Jesus Christ. As Christians, Christ enables us to live as people who minister in His name. Deacons receive this same charge. Because of this, deacons perform their ministry as servants of the Lord to the church.

Harold opened his Bible and read to Shannon 1 Timothy 3:8-13. This text highlights the qualities needed by persons who wish to serve as deacons.

- Christian dedication. The word *grave* (see 1 Tim. 3:8) has as its meaning "respect for Christ's teachings. "
- Truthfulness in speech. Not "double-tongued' (see 1 Tim. 3:8) describes a person whose speech can be trusted to be truthful.

• Disciplined Christian living. The phrases "not given to much wine" and "not greedy of filthy lucre" (1 Tim. 3:8) admonish deacons to be disciplined in their conduct. A deacon's decision about the sale or use of alcoholic beverages should be made on the basis of influence. Will a deacon's decision lead other people closer to Christ? A deacon's attitude about money and material possessions should bring honor to Christ.

• Integrity in Christian conduct. "Holding the mystery of the faith with a clear conscience" (1 Tim. 3:9) means that a deacon's life-style should reflect a sincere effort to keep the teachings of Christ.

• Proven spiritual maturity. "Proved" (1 Tim. 3:10) means "tested." The deacon should be a person whose spiritual maturity has been proved.

• Christian family life. First Timothy 3:12 points out that a deacon must demonstrate commitment to the sanctity of marriage vows. In his home, a deacon is a leader who advocates Christian teachings and loving relationships.[1]

Each congregation determines roles.—Deacons serving in Baptist churches are governed by Baptist understandings of the church and by Baptist polity. The church exists not as an organization but as an organism. This statement means a church consists of people. As deacons do their work, the needs of people become their priority. Deacon work involves helping people come to know Christ, nurturing them in their spiritual growth, and assisting them to become involved meaningfully in the life of the church.

Additionally the church functions autonomously in regard to the Southern Baptist Convention. Each church has responsibility in deciding the qualifications, election procedures, and responsibilities of its deacons. The Southern Baptist Convention does not ordain anyone. Each local church has the responsibility for doing this. Deacon qualifications may vary from church to church, but in each case qualifications need to be based on those found in 1 Timothy 3:8-13.

The Holy Spirit gives direction.—As deacons accomplish their ministry, they do so with the understanding it is the

Spirit who tells them when, where, how, and to whom they are to give ministry.

Deacons perform their ministry role in cooperation with others in the church.—As Shannon listened to all of this, she began to wonder, *If deacons have the responsibility to do ministry, just what does that include?* Harold was only too happy to help her with the answer. He told her that the word *ministry* in its verb form comes from the Greek word *diakoneo*. He helped her understand ministry by giving her the following definition. "Ministry is individual, redemptive, loving service given inside and outside the church under the leadership of the Holy Spirit which meets people's needs and fulfills the church's mission."[2]

They also serve in a partnership with all others who help lead the church. This includes other deacons, the pastor, staff, Church Council members, and those who serve as leaders in the various church organizations and members of the various church committees.

As a partner, the deacon walks alongside the pastor and staff of the church. They work together in ministering to needs of the congregation and helping the church accomplish the purpose for which God led it to be established. Pastor, staff, and deacons work best together when their relationship is one of friendship as well as partnership.

Deacons perform three major tasks.—"So," said Shannon, "deacons do their work not as a board of directors or as a group of business managers, but as ministers."

"That's right," agreed Harold. "Three major tasks are central in effective deacon work."[3]

• One task is leading the church to accomplish its mission. The work of deacons involves leadership. To accomplish their leadership role, deacons serve as examples to the church, as faithful participants in the church's life, and as catalysts for appropriate change within the church.

• Another task is proclaiming the gospel to believers and unbelievers. This task includes witnessing to the lost, being involved in outreach activities, discipling the saved, participating in baptism and the Lord's Supper, and preaching when it is appropriate. Deacons carry out this task through concern for the outreach program of the church, the mission program of the church, and the worship services of the church.

• The third task is caring for church members and others persons in the community. Through activities such as the Deacon Family Ministry Plan, Deacon of the Week, meeting the benevolence needs of the church and community, deacons carry out this valuable task area.

As Shannon listened intently to all that had been shared with her, she began to realize deacons occupy an important place in the life of the church. She saw them as spiritual leaders who serve in partnership with the pastor and others in the congregation to enable the church to be successful. She came to understand that Zachary would be undertaking a ministry which would involve him in some time-consuming activities. She thought about her need to share him with the church. She also knew he would need to continue to learn and grow as a Christian and in the skills necessary for him to do his work effectively as a deacon. As she understood this, she also realized her vital place in this ministry of serving the Lord through the church.

Her Role
As she began to think about her own role in deacon ministry, Shannon thought about the deacons' wives in the church. She knew that these women were involved with their husbands' ministries in many ways. She had seen some as they were visible in ministry: preparing and serving meals, witnessing, and greeting newcomers. Often they served on committees and had leadership roles in Sunday School, Discipleship Training, music, and missions. She knew there were times when these women went with their husbands to visit people at home and in the hospitals. She also knew that others stayed in the background, assisting with Lord's Supper preparation, baptism, and praying. No two were alike. Although the church seemed to have some expectations for deacons' wives, there was room

for individuality. Would she be able to be herself? Could she express ministry through her own personality and exercise her own gifts?

Shannon wanted to understand more fully what her role in ministry should be. She asked Harold if he thought his wife, Nancy, would be willing to talk with her. "I'm sure she would be more than happy to give you a wife's point of view. Nancy can share some of her experiences with you," was his reply. Shannon made a telephone call and set up a meeting.

Shannon was soon put at ease as the wife of this deacon recalled some of her special ministry opportunities. "I wish I had sat down with the wife of a deacon early in my own experience," Nancy lamented. "It might have saved me some frustration. For a long time, I thought I had to be supermom and superwife. I tried to live up to the expectations everyone had for me. I thought I should teach a Sunday School class, lead a Discipleship Training group, sing in the choir, lead a children's choir, work with Mission Friends, attend Baptist Women, help in the library, teach in extended sessions for preschoolers during worship, serve on committees, feed the youth at their fellowships, visit the hospitals and nursing homes, and more!"

Nancy suggested that the role of a deacon's wife could best be summed up in two ways. First, Shannon would need to support Zachary in his ministry. Second, Shannon could minister alongside him at times. Carl and Martha Nelson's book, *The Ministering Couple,*[4] had been helpful to her. She also suggested *Equipping Deacons in Caring Skills.*[5]

Shannon's support would take many forms. She admired Zachary's commitment and had faith in him and his work as a deacon. But for Zachary to be at his best in ministry, she and others in their family needed to allow him to minister. Zachary needed to know his family was willing to share him. He needed to know that they were not only proud of him, but that they considered this ministry important. The family needed to understand that Zachary was following what he believed was the Lord's will for his life. What better example was there for children! As they grow older, it will be a logical thing for them to listen also to the Holy Spirit as He works in their lives.

The Bible shapes our understanding.—Shannon knew that 1 Timothy 3:11 contained some instructions directed to wives of deacons. This verse makes clear that the Lord's work is not to be taken lightly. The wife needs to share her husband's serious outlook on his ministry as a deacon. Because of the way she conducts herself, the deacon's wife needs to inspire respect. She needs to be self-controlled and trustworthy. Shannon knew she would need to continue to grow spiritually.

Gifts and interests focus your role.—Nancy went on to explain that in her earlier days as a deacon's wife she wasn't ministering; she was spinning her wheels. For her to realize she could best serve in the boundaries of her own personality, with her own gifts, and in her own time constraints took time. By spreading herself too thin, she wasn't doing her best in any one area. She finally understood that she wasn't the only one in the church who could take care of things that needed to be done.

As an example, Nancy explained she loved four- and five-year-olds. She loved her own children when they were that age. But after two weeks as a leader of Mission Friends, she knew that was *not* where she needed to be. Nancy was trying to fill a spot that could be better filled by another person.

Responsibilities require that you balance priorities.— Nancy offered Shannon this word of caution: Don't let your family feel that Zachary's commitment to ministry is pushing them aside. A balance of priorities must exist. This means that it will sometimes be necessary to make personal sacrifices. Plans might need to be changed. Sometimes interruptions will occur. Occasionally he will be late. You and Zachary must have good communication so that his concerns can become your concerns. You and Zachary will need to share goals. You will need to talk about attitudes, likes, and dislikes. Help him keep his ministry opportunities in perspective. Don't let deacon work come before your family, but don't let your family become an excuse not to minister.

Circumstances impact your responses.—Nancy told Shannon about an incident that happened recently. "A friend was out of town when there was a crisis in a family in her church. When she returned home several weeks later, she visited the family. She found that while many people had been attentive at first, no one had called or gone by to visit in quite some time. This friend told me that she now makes it a practice to put a notation on her husband's calendar for follow-up visits. Holidays, birthdays, and anniversaries are difficult for people who have experienced such a crisis. Don't assume that someone else is ministering. Be sensitive to needs."

Zachary would not be able to share some information with Shannon. He should be able to relax in the fact that she would not be jealous or feel left out. During the times he needed to share information with her, he would rely on her to keep confidences. She needed to be a good listener.

Your touch enriches his ministry.—Shannon realized she would need to help Zachary keep track of ministry opportunities. Because of demands on his time, she saw the importance of helping him plan ways to maximize the quality of family time and cope with demands on him. She could help him keep a calendar of ministry opportunities. She could make notations of birthdays, anniversaries, and other dates special to those to whom he would minister. At times she would learn of needs and be able to share these with him.

You can act independently.—Nancy reminded Shannon that many times deacons and their wives are hesitant to minister because they are afraid they won't know what to say in particular situations. She had found that the ministry of presence was valuable. Sometimes there was no need to say anything—just be there.

One other thing Nancy had found to be important was to be specific. She recently talked with the young mother of a new baby. She almost made the mistake of saying, "If there is anything I can do, let me know." A more appropriate statement would be, "May I keep your baby for you while you run some errands?" or "May I run some errands for you?" Sometimes she called one of the ladies who had difficulty getting out and told this lady that she was on her way to the grocery. Did she need anything? There were times when the offer of help should be general? However, people are often hesitant to call and ask for help. She reminded Sharon to be careful not to intrude or embarrass anyone. An offer to do laundry or clean the kitchen might cause hard feelings.

Many wives of deacons love to cook. They feel they can minister through their kitchen. Some double a recipe and have a casserole to share. When they make a batch of cookies or a cake, they take some to a shut-in or a lonely person. One person doesn't need the whole cake. In fact, one friend who loves to cook only has herself and her husband to cook for since her children are grown and away. She keeps a small portion for her husband and herself and gives the large portion to a family where both father and mother work outside the home.

Other women are more comfortable ministering in other ways. Some spend time with shut-ins or people in nursing homes. Others draw newcomers into the fellowship of the church. One deacon's wife said her favorite ministry is in assisting with baptism. She doesn't seem to notice the wet towels and baptismal clothing. The expressions on the faces of people following their baptism makes it all worthwhile.

Nancy suggested that Shannon's family could participate in ministry by praying for Zachary as he visited people who were sick, in sorrow, in crises, or lost. Zachary could depend on their prayer support as he answered questions about his faith and about their church.

She would need to encourage him at times when he would be tired or feel overwhelmed by his responsibilities. She would need to affirm his gifts and help him find his own special way to minister.

Their Role
As Shannon thought of ways she could minister alongside Za-

chary, she was reminded of the differences in his gifts and her gifts. Rather than this being a problem, she began to see this as an advantage. She realized his strengths and her strengths would lead to many ministry opportunities. Still, she was aware that he was the one who had been chosen to be a deacon and that she was his helpmate.

Share ministry.—A deacon and his wife form a partnership to use their gifts, interests, and resources for ministry through their church. As Shannon thought of the team relationship, she realized that she and Zachary would need to be sensitive to one another. They would need to accept the uniqueness of one another.

Grow together.—One thing Shannon was sure of—she and Zachary would need to continue to grow spiritually in order to minister effectively. She knew that their daily Bible study and prayer would be essential. She also knew that growth could sometimes be painful. She recalled times in their lives when trouble had caused them to rely totally on the Lord.

Shannon and Zachary would need to help each other to minister without burning out. They would need to take time to shape their ministry.

Visit together.—As Shannon and Zachary would go about their daily activities, she knew that they would have opportunities to share their faith with non-Christians. At times Shannon would accompany Zachary as he visited with families who had attended their church and were looking for a church home. Together they would be able to show the kind of caring fellowship that existed in the congregation.

For her to accompany Zachary as he had opportunities to minister in the homes of women would be important. Together they could visit the hospitals and nursing homes.

They would be able to express to church members and nonmembers what their church was all about. They could share about missions. They would have to know what they believed. As a team they would need to uphold the programs of the church, as well as those in leadership positions.

Shannon and Zachary as a team would be able to personalize the love of God in many ways. She would be able to assist him in his caring role. Together they would be able to express care to families in the congregation. They could minister in times of stress or sorrow. They could offer counsel or refer people to someone who could help.

Shannon remembered how comforting it was to her when a deacon and his wife ministered to her during a time of crisis in her own life. This couple had rejoiced with Shannon and Zachary when their children were born. They had encouraged them when they were seeking ways to serve in and through their church. The deacon and his wife felt a freedom to minister in a time of crisis because they had established a relationship with Shannon and Zachary during good times.

Know and support your church.—For them to know of the activities and ministries of their church would be important. In dealing with newcomers and visitors to their church, Shannon and Zachary would need to answer questions about the time and place of activities for the entire family. Was child care provided during choir practice? When did GAs and RAs meet (or did they meet at all)? What special activities were available for young people during the week and on Sundays? How could new members be brought into the fellowship of the church?

They and other deacon couples would provide a stability in the life of the church by being faithful, willing, and available. During times of conflict, they could have a calming influence. When the church might be without a pastor or other staff member, they could show faithfulness to the activities and worship opportunities.

Be an example.—Their family would show patterns of Christian family life. They could demonstrate, not the perfect family life, but a family seeking to follow biblical principles. Shannon and Zachary could be an example by working through difficult times. Their faithfulness to worship and Bible study should be a model for others.

Shannon recognized that she and Zachary could be key people in developing a caring church fellowship. They would encourage people to participate in social occasions. As a couple Shannon and Zachary would be able to help families develop respect for their pastor, staff, and other church leaders. They could help others find ways to use their gifts to serve through the church.

Shannon reminded herself that she and Zachary each had individual gifts. However, their togetherness as husband and wife would add to their effectiveness. Because Shannon and Zachary came from different backgrounds, they each added a special dimension to ministry. Their life experiences gave each of them insights into different situations.

Some ministry opportunities would be planned, organized projects that might be for a short or long period of time. Others might be a spontaneous response to a current situation. Many opportunities would involve maintaining a high level of caring and ministry to the fellowship of believers in their church.

Shannon thought about the amount of time she and Zachary had available for ministry. She realized that, as their family grew, their time priorities would change. She thought of the hectic routine of couples with young children and those with teenagers. She thought of the time availability of couples whose children had moved away from home. She thought of retired couples. She reminded herself that commitment to ministry is not for a 30-day period but is a way of life.

She realized that working alongside her deacon husband would be a way to center her attention away from her own personal interests. She thought of the sense of purpose, well-being, and personal satisfaction they would both feel. She knew that following in Jesus' steps in ministry would bring God's "well done" to their lives.

[1]Adapted from Robert Sheffield, *The Ministry of Baptist Deacons* (Nashville: Convention Press, 1990), 37-41.

[2]Ibid., 15-16.

[3]Ibid., 32.

[4]Carl and Martha Nelson, *The Ministering Couple* (Nashville: Broadman Press, 1983).

[5]Homer D. Carter, *Equipping Deacons in Caring Skills* (Nashville: Convention Press, 1980).

Barbara Sheffield is a middle-school teacher, free-lance writer, and conference leader for deacons' wives. She lives in Nashville, Tennessee.

Chapter 2

Time Enough for Violets

Faye Wellborn Robbins

The straw that broke the camel's back came one Sunday morning. My husband, whose job frequently takes him out of town, started to go just as I was getting ready for Sunday School. I hastily threw on the new dress he had bought for my birthday so he could see it before leaving. After a quick kiss that landed somewhere near his ear, I waved a hurried good-bye and, with scarcely a pause, grabbed the choir anthem I had brought home to memorize. Adding my Bible, offering envelope, *Adult Teacher*, and purse, I rushed out to my car, herding my 13-year-old son before me. We drove the 12 miles to church and spent several minutes finding a parking place. Up to that point, it had been an ordinary, run-of-the-mill Sunday morning.

No Longer Run-of-the-Mill

As I struggled out of the enveloping bucket seat, I felt something strike my leg. To my amazed horror, I discovered on my skirt one of those magnetic devices some stores brad to their clothes to foil shoplifters. At the moment it seemed singularly ineffective. The clerk must have absent-mindedly wrapped it up in the box with the dress. I sent my son into Sunday School and frantically tried to pry it loose. After three broken fingernails, a bent nail file, and a scratched car key, I gave up. I could only hope that no one would notice my skirt and think I had stolen it.

Later, as I looked at my class members, I wondered how many of them experienced the same kind of time-related stress I did.

Secretly, I pushed the two-inch clothes tag further under my knee. With a husband, a just-turned teenager, a teaching job, a house to care for, occasional writing assignments, some social obligations and some just-for-pleasure-ones, as well as church demands to be met, I never seemed to have the time to do anything really well.

Now my husband had been elected a deacon. As much as he traveled, I knew he would ask me to take up the slack when necessary. How could I do it all? Obviously anyone who would go to church sporting a quarter of a pound shoplifters alarm on the side of her dress either had a severe mental disturbance, or else she was just too hurried, too harried, too busy.

The Problem Was Wide-spread

As the class visited together a few minutes before I began the lesson, I could hear snatches of conversation going on around me.

"Someone asked me to teach a class next church year, but I had to tell them I just did not have time."

"The kids wanted me to take some refreshments to school for their class party, but I am just too tired at night to add anything extra to what I already do."

"I know that book you mentioned is a good one. I wish I had time to read."

The same story was heard from every corner of the room. No one had enough time. Max Lucado captured the essence of the problem when he said, "We're the only nation on earth with a mountain called 'Rushmore.' "[1] With all the time-saving devices like the microwave, the computer, the washing machine, and the dryer (I cherish them all with the possible exception of the bulky microwave) that crowd our houses, we are busier than ever.

What the Questionnaires Showed

Before writing this chapter, I sent out some questionnaires to help me prepare. All who filled them out gave me the same message. You indicated, directly or indirectly, that you felt you did not have enough time together as a family. The words, "the demands of the church," appeared several times along with the warning to guard oneself and one's family against them. I do not think this indicates any lack of love for the church. I think it is the distress cry of people so rushed that they must clamor up a rising, airport escalator two steps at a time to make the plane while stuffing last-minute papers into a briefcase.

How to Thrive, Not Just Survive

The embarrassing dress incident happened sometime ago, but it made me stop and reassess my life. In the process, I believe I have learned a few principles that have helped simplify my life and make it possible to thrive, not just survive. Oh, my world still gets too crowded and the tasks pile up at times. Then I stop and remind myself of some things I already know. You probably know them, too, but like me you may profit from a few reminders.

Something I Learned in the Kitchen

When I was growing up, dishwashers in our house consisted of my sister and me. Since my mother was known for her generous hospitality, we sometimes thought she had given us insurmountable tasks. We tried to make our point by adding up how many dishes we would have to wash in our lifetime at the rate we were going. Mother put a stop to our wails by telling us we were making unnecessary trouble for ourselves. The right way to manage this chore was to meet the future when it came. For now, wash the dishes one meal at a time. We could, she was sure, manage that much.

She was wiser than she knew, for the electric dishwasher in my kitchen has reduced that old task to a minimum. The principle, however, remains valid. Without cluttering my mind with the entire future, I do, one at a time, the jobs I set for myself that day. This means of prioritizing is something like putting the clean dishes away on the shelves. When evening comes, the dish rack is empty. The next day there is new energy; new strength; and a whole, glorious, new stretch of 24 hours in which to be alive. Stop worrying about what you have lined up to do all week. Just wash the dishes one meal at a time.

Something I Learned from Daylight Savings

I have a second suggestion. Whatever your responsibilities,

scheduling is helpful. Now, obviously, we have no control over when Thanksgiving comes or PTA meets. Meals must be served somewhat regularly, baths must be taken, and time clocks must be punched. I am thinking of those extra commitments which crowd our days. This is where creativity in time management comes in.

The best way I know to maximize the hours available is to set reasonable deadlines and then meet them ahead of time. This may involve some awkwardness at the beginning, but it can be done. Have you ever noticed that when we change our clocks in the fall and again in the spring because of daylight saving, the difficulties of readjustment are only momentary? We simply move everything forward—or back—one hour and continue as we planned. Do that same trick on a personal basis and see what happens. You will feel the most incredible lift when you look at your finished job and see that it is not due today but next week.

If this sounds like madness to you when every day is a hassle, there is method in it. This kind of timing allows for that unexpected interruption that comes to all of us, sometimes tragically.

My mother, who lived eight hundred miles away, was quite ill. The end of the semester was near; and in college teaching that is when term papers are due, finals must be prepared, grades must be readied for averaging, failing students must be counseled, and final lectures must be prepared to give the student every chance to do well. My habit has long been to get as much of that done ahead of time as possible, partly to take some of the load off the department secretary.

Probably because I was worried about my mother, I made out my final exams early that year and prepared my grades so that only the last exam had to be averaged in. On the eve of the final day of lectures my mother died, and we had to leave as soon as I could get out of class the next day. It was, of course, a difficult time, but having my teaching affairs in order made it easier. That experience reinforced my conviction that it is wise and actually much less trouble if you provide a buffer time zone in your schedule to allow for the unexpected.

Something I Learned from a College Roommate

I had a roommate in college who never made the grades she wished. I listened to her sympathetically and tried to talk with her tactfully about her study habits. Nothing I said made any difference. She always studied a long time, she said, for every test. Well, she did put in a lot of time. I have watched her open her history book and stare steadily at it for at least 10 minutes. Then she would get her nail polish and proceed to work on her nails while she studied. When that was done, she would fiddle with the radio until she found the station she wanted. While she looked at her notes, her lips moved to the words of the song being played. In those days we rolled our hair every night, and putting in those rollers would be her next task. Upon completing the three hours she considered the reasonable amount any test should require, she put away her notes. She had indeed accomplished many things, none of which, unfortunately, contributed much to answering the questions she would face the next day. She had spent three hours with a book open before her; she had not studied.

Watching her taught me the necessity of centering my entire attention on the task at hand. That meant disciplining my mind to keep it from roaming throughout the universe at the same time. Other responsibilities would be there when I was ready for them. Meanwhile, the job I had chosen for this segment of time would be truly accomplished. I could put it away without worry.

Something I Learned at PraiSing II

In March 1991, thousands of Southern Baptists gathered in the Opry House in Nashville to celebrate and dedicate *The Baptist Hymnal*. Wesley Forbis, director of the Church Music Department of the Sunday School Board and editor of the new hymnal, took a few minutes to remember James Woodward of Oklahoma. Just weeks earlier, Jim and several others were killed in an airplane crash. He was to have directed the congregational singing that evening. In a moving tribute, Forbis acknowledged the presence of Betty, Jim's wife. She was, Forbis said, Jim's inspiration and his special joy because she allowed him space to realize his creativity.

So your husband is a deacon, and it often takes him away from home at night. You may be ashamed to say it out loud, but sometimes you resent those meetings, those hours he spends at the church. He should be with the family. He should be home with you. Or should he?

A healthy family life is more than being under the same roof at the same time. To me, the essence of love is concern for the welfare of the beloved. That includes being willing for each family member to do God's will and to follow his own star. Does your husband feel called to serve his Lord through being a deacon? Being a deacon takes time and work. Surely the husband and father contributes much to his family when he models unselfish service and dependable commitment to the cause of the Kingdom. Surely the wife and mother sets a noble pattern for family members when she puts her own concerns second to those of her loved ones.

Does it cost to follow this path? Yes. Is it worth it? I think so. I would like for someone one day to say of me that I gave my husband and son space to realize their creativity and their calling and by doing so gave them joy.

Redeeming the Time of Our Life

Sometimes our problem with time management lies, not in the demands, but in ourselves. The following are some lessons I learned about time management.

Something I Learned at the Piano

In my childhood, the piano was my mortal enemy! Every new piece was a struggle, every practice session a trial, and every recital a black misery. In spite of all that, or maybe because of all that, perhaps nothing so enhances life for me as music.

Practicing became less tedious as the meaning of the black characters on sheet music became less obscure. The learning process took time. When, for instance, I finally came to understand the function of the rest, it was rewarding.

The choir is performing. The rest appears on the staff, and the voices stop. The conductor, however, continues to beat the time with unvarying count. He will bring the choir back in at the right moment as if no break had occurred. The rest gives the performer time to catch his breath; but more, it serves as a comma, a semicolon, or a period in a sentence. The rest is, then, a device used by the composer to allow the music line to make sense. It is absolutely necessary to the development, the importance, and the beauty of the melody. The rest has no music in it, but there is the *making* of music in it.

The rest has the same important function in the music of our lives. We may need to take time to pause and make sense of it all. We may need to rest and not feel guilty.

Sometimes, however, sickness, deep grief, disappointment, frustrated efforts, or unexpected setbacks can force us into a time of unwanted leisure. Everything comes to a dead halt, and our days appear meaningless. Whatever song our hearts were singing becomes completely silent. We may feel that we have come to the end of the theme.

If that has happened to you, remember that God is the Master Conductor. He is still counting out the time. He never misses a beat. If we learn to rest in the Lord and look to Him, we will find we can sound the next notes full and clear. Don't waste the rests in your life even if they come unsought and unwanted. They can be times of renewal and refreshment. They can give added richness to your whole life melody. In God's time, the song goes on.

Something I Learned from a Busy Person

D. C. Applegate was pastor of First Baptist Church, Starkville, Mississippi, for 17 years, beginning in 1954. During those years he managed that most delicate of tasks for a university church pastor. He was able to preach in a meaningful way to both students and townspeople without slighting either. As important as he considered the pulpit, his work there was only one part of his ministry. He and his wife, Kate, opened their home to towns-people and students alike. Each Christmas, they routinely entertained groups of more than four hundred guests before the season was past.

Like all pastors, he responded to telephone calls day and night. The calls took him or both him and Kate to the bedsides of ill church members as well as strangers. Sometime, it was to the campus.

The students of Mississippi State were special people to the Applegates. The Applegates not only entertained the students in their home, they also taught and counseled them at all hours. They ministered to them in times of illness or grief and went to them whenever they called. To catch a glimpse of Kate and D. C. Applegate on the campus at 10:30 at night was a common sight. Each would be running to a dormitory or fraternity house for devotions.

Under Applegate's loving leadership and ministry, the church grew steadily. Then in the midst of the most fruitful years of his pastorate, D. C. Applegate was diagnosed with multiple sclerosis. The stunned church, recognizing what the future held for them all, began to plan and act. Realizing that climbing stairs at the three-storied pastorium would soon be impossible for their pastor, they built the family a special house. Its doors were six inches wider than usual to accommodate the inevitable wheelchair. The slanted shower floor made it possible for him to roll into position. Many exits guaranteed that one would always be readily accessible in case of fire.

In the spring of 1968, Applegate, his wife, and daughter moved into this house that love built. Members of past as well as the current congregation helped provide for their comfort and care. Not to be left out were a number of former students who had found in "Preacher" a model of Christian life and faith. He had been to them an encourager, a direction-giver, a mentor.

Death came to D. C. Applegate when he was in his late eighties. Many of those "adopted" children whose lives had been eternally changed under his ministry immediately reached out to Kate. In their love and gratitude, they have kept her aware she is not forgotten. I know. My husband is one of them.

You may find yourself growing weary in well-doing, especially if others seem to take you for granted. If no one appears to notice or care about all you do, remember the Applegates. Christian love is alive and well. The writer of Ecclesiastes spoke an important truth when he wrote, "Cast thy bread upon the waters: for thou shalt find it after many days" (Eccl. 11:1). Like an echo, the love we send out has a way of rebounding back on us. No recession ever affects the investment we make in the lives of others. It's the law of the harvest.

Something I Learned on a Mountain

A hazard exists even here. Sometimes our lives become so cluttered with all the things we do, we lose sight of the things that are! We look around us and wonder if this is all there is. Let me tell you of an experience I had.

Four of us were hiking in the Swiss Alps, hoping to catch a glimpse of the famed Matterhorn. We had been warned by the natives that seeing the mountain was highly unlikely that time of year. The mists lay heavily around us all day and seemed to prove them correct. Giving up, we turned toward the inn where we were staying, not at all certain there really was a Matterhorn after all. Suddenly, the sun came blazing forth, and there it was! Not only were we awestruck by its majesty but also by the sheer fact of its existence. All day the world had appeared empty. But that was wrong. The Matterhorn had been there all the time.

Sometimes it is like that with God. We get completely enveloped by the clouds of everyday tasks. We walk with our heads down, obsessed by the path we are treading, seeing only the rocks and the fog. We are not sure where we are going, and we feel a long way from home. Since we cannot see God or feel His presence, we may almost doubt that He is there. But He always is.

Lift up your eyes. Help is available—a Presence, a Strength, a Companion for your journey. No matter that for a moment the mists hide His face. He will never leave you or forsake you. He has promised that. In a little while, the sun will come out, and you will see Him again. Until then, believe it.

Something I Learned from a Jonquil

One of the things we as wives and mothers do in these busy days is make memories. The memories we wish to create are ones that will one day warm the hearts of those who remember us. We do that through our mothering, our home-making, our professional lives, and our church work. We also do it simply by being who we are.

Among the flowers that bloom early in our part of the country is the daffodil. These beautiful, yellow flowers are the harbingers of spring. Since they may begin blooming anytime from the first of March to the end of the month, they are sometimes called March flowers. One variety is called jonquils.

Their early blooming has been known to be followed by a heavy snow. Seeing their yellow heads sticking up above that blanket of white is especially appealing. The snow does not kill them. March flowers are going to "do their thing" after they bloom, no matter what. On their slender stems they look fragile, but they are not. They have endurance, and they have an innate sense of the appropriate. They know when it is the right time—no matter that cold winds may blow up; no matter that ice may rain from the sky; no matter that dark clouds may obscure the sun. They know that spring is just around the corner. The earth will grow warm, the breeze become gentle, and the sky turn blue. In spite of how things may appear to others, the daffodil is going to bloom and lift our hearts—not just this spring but on and on.

I remember going with my husband and his parents to his grandmother's farm. The grandparents were both dead. The old house had burned, and only the chimney remained standing. The land was being sold for a housing development expanding from Memphis.

My father-in-law took a slow stroll around what had been the front yard and paused by the jonquils growing near what had been the front steps. His mother had put them there when she came as a bride. He bent and carefully dug up the bulbs. "We'll plant these at home," he said. He did. Now every March they bloom again around another doorstep, giving renewed pleasure and something else—a kind of reassurance that life holds something permanently lovely for the willing spirit.

A beauty exists that endures, is reliable, and pulls at the heartstrings because it is tied up with memories that are precious treasures of the mind.

Sometime it is necessary to leave behind the deadlines, bills, dishes, car pool and go where the jonquils bloom. Behold the enduring, the indomitable, the beautiful. Look on the face of God. You will come back refreshed in spirit and ready again to make a precious memory for those you love.

Something I Learned on My Knees

According to the answers to my questionnaire, being a deacon's wife can be a cause for pride or frustration. Being a deacon's wife can add insight into the workings of the church and staff relationships. To some it was a source of growth, a new consciousness of being a Christian example. Sometimes it evoked jealousy, sometimes indifference. Some viewed it as as just another church job. To some it was an opportunity for Christian service.

The different attitudes seem to be closely related to the view of one's own calling. I found mine on my knees in my prayer closet and in a familiar verse of Scripture. The Scripture says, "Seek ye first the kingdom of God, and his righteousness; and all these things shall be added unto you" (Matt. 6:33).

I believe that means we are to seek God and His will before all else. We are to seek God before personal desires, professional demands, possessions, success, even before family. The emphasis here seems to be a matter of priority. Certainly it does not mean that we are to ignore profession, family, provision for the necessities of life, or even our personal desires. Certainly it does not mean that we are to disregard the children He has given into our care. They are human souls we are to nurture while we can. These babies are born. We turn around, and they are the adults we have helped to fashion. We can never go back and undo what we did or failed to do.

Everything God has provided for our good and happiness has its proper place. Danger comes when we choose to rearrange the order.

Our calling is first to that primary relationship with our Heavenly Father. We are to know Him, to love Him, and to obey Him. He leads us all in different paths, but He has a path for each of us. Our business is to discover that path and to accept God's will as our own.

Sometimes that is hard, but always it is best. Remember, this is not the will of a despot we are being called to accept. We are being called to accept the will of the best of fathers for a dearly loved child.

We can be sure of this. That assurance is inherent in the new name Jesus gave us for God. Jesus taught us to call God "Father" when we pray. In Bethlehem, in Nazareth, in Galilee, in the garden of Gethsemane, on the cross of Calvary, Jesus spelled out this new name for us. The name speaks the truth we learned in early Sunday School—that God is love. We can safely seek Him first, for He wants only our highest good. Having our priorities straight will eliminate many questions that would otherwise rise to plague us.

Something I Learned from a Bout with Cancer

A few years ago I became seriously ill. Our household suffered a time of great stress. For me it was a time of reexamination. After severe surgery to remove the cancer, I experienced a long recovery period. My primary emotion was one of gratitude—for life, for family, for friends, for church, for the opportunities and beauty that had filled my life, and for the presence of God through it all.

Priorities were not changed, for I had settled those a long

time ago. The illness was a lesson, however, in the fragility of life on this earth. *Now* was important. I was reminded that death could come at any moment, and aspects of my life were left undone. Somehow, I did not want to go to the Father with unused gifts, unsaid thank you's, unspoken I love you's in my pocket.

I wrote letters of appreciation to people who had especially contributed to my life from childhood on. The words, *I love you*, have never, for some reason, come easily for me. Therefore, I needed to tell people dear to me that I loved them. I could not reach one person, but God has made that possible in the years since. Not everyone was waiting breathlessly to hear those words from me, of course. But I wanted to say them just in case it mattered at all. To some, it did matter.

Unrealized dreams and possibilities I had never taken time to explore were there. I remembered challenges I had never quite had the courage to meet. All in all, I was made dramatically aware that waiting can rob one of opportunity.

The first step in this priority business is to tell God He can do anything with our lives He wishes. However, this is only the beginning. We must then follow His guidance.

When the three men came to Abraham to inform him that Sarah would have a son, he understood. This was a visitation from God. Abraham offered them ready hospitality and received the blessing (see Gen. 18:2-14). I am afraid we are not always that alert. Many of us miss God's leadership simply because when He comes to us, He finds no welcome. We don't recognize Him. We are not looking.

Along with your commitment to being a good wife and mother, is there anything else God wants from you? Does He have a special way for you to express His primacy in your life? He has given you talents, yearnings, desires. Submit them to His will. If the dreams you have were born at Calvary, set about realizing them.

The opportunity to do so may be as familiar as teaching a Sunday School class. Supporting your husband wholeheartedly in his role as deacon may be an opportunity. Another opportunity may be taking up painting or playing the oboe. Vocational Christian service or teaching literacy classes may provide yet another opportunity. Whatever you do, offer it to God. Do it humbly to the Lord. "Whether therefore ye eat, or drink, or whatsoever ye do, do all to the glory of God" (1 Cor. 10:31).

We all have obligations, limitations, and boundaries in which we must function. We all also have the privilege of making some choices. A neat little heading on our computer advises us it will "clean up the window." Give the correct instruction, and it will do just that. Order comes out of disorder. You can see just what is actually in that computer. Sometimes we need to press that button in our lives and eliminate the clutter. We can take a good look at what we allow to push and pull us. We can then choose to concentrate on matters that have eternal significance. That makes it possible to redeem the time and really enjoy God's world.

My perspective has changed from those other days of hurry and hustle. The *moments* are precious today. They provide the gauge by which I measure life's joy. Look to the moment. We really don't have much time.

So brief the candle's glow,
The lilac's bloom,
The twilight's gentle balm!
So soon the snowflakes melt
Upon one's mouth,
The dew upon the lawn.

So write the poem;
Sing the song;
Walk barefoot through the sands.
For lesser things
Give love away, and
Hold violets in your hands.

[1]Max Lucado, *The Applause of Heaven* (Dallas: Word Publishing, 1990),18.

Faye Wellborn Robbins is a deacon's wife who lives in Nashville, Tennessee and who teaches an adult women's Sunday School class. She also is a university professor, a free-lance writer, and conference leader.

Chapter 3

Continuing to Grow

Fayly H. Cothern

She was six years old! In two weeks our pert, pony-tailed daughter would start school. The flurry of getting ready for the gigantic life step included taking up hems in new dresses and letting out hems in older ones.

One day as she stood before the floor-length mirror, trying to stay still long enough for me to mark the hemline, she exclaimed, "Oh, I'm so excited! I'm growing up!"

Every now and then as I assess myself in the spiritual mirror, I ask, "Am I still growing?" Then the next question is, "Is excitement still part and parcel of my growth?"

Commit the You God Called

Think back to the time you first heard that the church had chosen your husband as a deacon. How did you feel about how his call affected you? Many women have some difficulty at this point. We struggle with how to be a deacon's wife. We wonder what people expect of us. If there is an older deacon's wife whom we admire, we sometimes try to emulate her.

During college years I was elected president of the BSU. Frances, the graduating senior who had served so efficiently in that office, was one I admired. She was a quiet, gentle person. She walked with the Lord and inspired others to do so likewise. Several years later she became a foreign missionary.

In the weeks following the election I focused on Frances. The way she conducted business, the manner in which she dealt with others, and her personality traits became especially important to me as I observed her more intently.

After a couple of weeks, my roommate finally confronted me—in love.

"Roomie," she asked, "are you feeling OK?"

"Sure," I replied, "why do you ask?"

"Well, you're so different these days. You aren't yourself. You're so quiet—almost withdrawn. I've been afraid you might be ill, or something."

That jolted me back to reality. Taking my Bible and notepad, I headed for my retreat—a vine-covered porch on the administration building—an entrance not often used.

Be yourself.—In that quiet place, God allowed me to see that He uses people with differing personality traits, spiritual gifts and abilities to accomplish His work. The apostle Paul said, "There are varieties of service, but it is the same God who inspires them all in every one" (1 Cor. 12:5, RSV).[1] "The Lord assigned to each. I planted, Apollos watered, but God gave the growth" (1 Cor. 3:5-6, RSV).

With that insight, I could relax and just be me, the me God made and wanted to hone and polish for His use. All I had to do was be available and willing.

Do you suppose that lesson stuck? No. God has reaffirmed those principles and has added insights through the years.

For example, when my husband was ordained, I had trouble with spiritual gifts, and renewed concern about my personality traits. Suddenly I found myself feeling as though I should have all the gifts and a just-right personality to utilize them to the fullest.

I was a "Miz Piggie" long before the cute cartoon character made us laugh. My piggy attitude, though, was no laughing matter. I found myself *acting* as though I had some gifts just because it seemed to me that the wife of an ordained deacon should be a spiritual superwoman.

Need I even tell you that there was no joy in my ministry under such circumstances?

Once more God had to draw me to a quiet place and speak to me through His Word.

Biblical women weren't alike.—I took a look at Deborah

see Judg. 4:4). She certainly wasn't a shy, dependent woman who took a quiet backstage role. As a dominate, intelligent, assertive woman, God used her. As a woman of great faith and wisdom, God used her.

Combining all of her personality traits, talents, abilities, background experiences, and spiritual gifts, God used her total person. She became a counselor, judge, and deliverer. She trusted God and inspired others to trust Him.

Then there was Sarah (see Gen. 11:29—25:40), a beautiful woman who for a time even lived a lie for her husband at his request. Later, as an aggressive, determined woman she took God's matters into her own hands. She worked out a plan to have children, and it worked. Yet her shortcut brought suffering. Jealousy, bitterness, anger, and even near death for a boy and his mother resulted from Sarah's manipulations.

Yet in spite of her human weaknesses, God loved her and used her as one of his instruments. It was she who bore the son who would carry God's covenant through His chosen people.

Abigail, another beautiful woman, had the gift of wisdom and diplomacy (see 1 Sam.25:32-33). A caring, peace-loving person, she had to do her good deeds in spite of her husband's selfishness and gruff, abusive manner.

Then there was Priscilla (see 2 Tom.4:19). She worked alongside her husband, Aquila, as they made their living making tents.

The apostle Paul called her by a pet nickname, Prisca. He spoke of her with fondness, as a friend. Priscilla and Aquila shared the good news of Christ with nonbelievers. They taught new believers, including the preacher Apollos.

Their mission concerns even took them to Ephesus and Rome where they helped start house churches. Marketplace evangelism was their way of life.

Was Priscilla childless? Perhaps. The Scriptures don't answer that question for us. The important thing is that she allowed God to use her.

Ah! The many stories of biblical wives remind me that there is no need to try to play a role. God just wanted me to be me—the me He made. If I could remain available and willing, He would use me as one of His ministers in whatever way He chose.

Remember covenant with God.—Along with commitment of the self God made, we also need to reaffirm our initial covenant with God. Remember? We came to that time when we had to either believe or reject Christ. Once believing, we then faced constant decisions of whether to obey or rebel.

We still do, don't we? Growing spiritually involves continual renewal.

Just in case you are reading this and you don't have an absolute conviction that you belong to Christ, you need to ask Him to come into your life. He not only will be your Savior but also your Lord. The Spirit of God will dwell within you. Your personhood will become His temple.

After the *indwelling* of God in your life, then you will ask for an *infilling* of His spirit frequently. This is reaffirmation that you want God to fill every crack and crevice of your mind, your habits, your total self. In that way He possesses all of you as His minister. You will be His representative, a "little Christ," to the people in your circle of influence. Day by day, sometimes hourly, you make a conscious, deliberate choice of asking Him to assume full control and direction of your life.

Focus on the Father

Have you ever gotten ready for bed on Sunday night feeling completely zapped? I have lots of times. Pushing the mental replay button, I do a fast rerun of the day's tape: getting breakfast, helping the family get ready for church, teaching a Bible study class, choir and worship, emotional drain from dealing with people problems, lunch and dealing with family interpersonal relationships, a late afternoon meeting, evening worship, back at home again, getting things together for the family Monday morning exodus. End of tape.

Finally I've eased my weary body into the bed and thought, *Thank the Lord this day of rest is over.*

And that's just the first day of the week!

Most of us travel life in overdrive, don't we? Frequently our days are so pressure packed that we feel we're on a treadmill and can't get off. How on earth, then, do we manage continual spiritual growth when we're so busy just trying to keep up?

Deliberate, willful focus on the Father works. The days which begin with a mental focus on God are always better days because the pattern has been set.

Affirm His presence.—Before getting out of bed, I thank God for His presence and protection. Reaffirming my belief in His saving power, I ask Him to fill my life anew with His Spirit. Then I ask Him to use me as His instrument—His conduit—to share the good news of Jesus, both in word and in deed, with those who cross my path during the day.

It is an amazing and exciting adventure to see how God engineers things so that those He wants to reach make contact with us. Often seeming "happenstance" encounters turn out to be God's doing.

Sometimes He prompts people to call on the phone. Still other times they come to our door. Many times we become involved with people whom we laughingly call "baskets on our doorstep." We marvel at how many people run out of gas in front of our house. Many a can of lawn mower fuel has helped get people to a station, along with a word or encouragement and a witness of God's concern. We keep tracts at our front door. Often we feel impressed to share one of them.

Focusing on God in the morning helps us when we're faced with the many decisions which arise. We are able to sift options through the grid of "what would Jesus do?" Always it is possible to consult *the* authority. God is absolute. His word is our guidebook.

Not only is life improved with the right beginning of each morning, but taking time during the day to refocus adds to the quality of living. During the rush of days filled with many responsibilities, it is easy to forget our primary purpose as children of God. We are to glorify Him with the way we live out our lives. One way to glorify Him is with praise.

Praise Him.—Friends of ours have developed a habit of putting a praise tape on their player each morning. As they get ready for the day's activities, the words of praise songs fill the house. Often they sing along.

Another friend is a whistler. Throughout the day, when circumstances are so that she can whistle, she trills melodies to songs which affirm God's love.

Some people sing their praise. Others hum. Still others "voice " praise to God from the quietness of their hearts. The important thing is to praise Him. There truly is power in praise.

Do you have those sleepless nights when your mind keeps mulling over problems? Try praise. One way to keep the mind focused on praise is to start down the alphabet finding adjectives which describe God. Such as: Father God, you are almighty, you are bountiful, you are caring, you are. . . .

Then to think that He cares for you!

The story has been told many times of a man who was recognized as a great theologian and teacher. After many years of study, someone asked him, "What is the most important thing you have learned about God?" To which he answered, "That Jesus loves me!"

We can relate to that, can't we? And we can praise Him, for He is indeed worthy of praise.

Schedule Time to Spend with God

In addition to the brief times when we turn our thoughts to the Lord, we need some time alone with God. Only through study of God's Word and conversing with Him in prayer can we have continuing spiritual growth.

With most people involved in the clamor of today's world, time with the Lord must be scheduled in the same way we calendarize most of our lives. We make our lists—a time to buy groceries, get our hair done, see the doctor, and all the other things necessary to our existence. Sometimes the "to do" list seems like a giant hour-eating monster.

Long ago my husband and I learned that if we didn't

schedule time for each other and for family, our available hours would be taken up by other people or by less important tasks.

The same is true of our relationship with God. A good way of assessing our priorities is taking a look at our calendar of scheduled tasks and appointments. To have quality time with the Lord, we often must say no to some things. Frequently those things are important. Often they involve some aspect of ministry. Yet which is *most* important?

Each of us must work out a time which is best for our prayer and learning time with the Lord. Mothers with small children at home have limited options compared to a retired woman. If the priority is high enough, however, the determination to find a time will prevail.

Once you've worked out your best time, look for a place which is most conducive for prayer and study. If at all possible, use that same place for your "prayer closet" each day.

I found that my desk was not a good spot for me because I was so easily distracted by the "to do" stack.

Our bedroom proves best for my quiet time. Beside a comfortable chair is a small bookcase which holds several translations and paraphrases of the Bible. Several books, including a concordance, Bible dictionary, and harmony of the Gospels, are "in residence." A notebook, pen, and prayer list are standard equipment.

Prayer.—Although some individuals prefer Bible study before prayer, my personal preference is prayer first. Prayer helps me focus on the Father. After a time of adoration, praise, and thanksgiving, I can make necessary confession. This unloads the emotional baggage which takes thought and energy better used for other things.

This confession time often reveals things from the past which motivate me or cause me to react in less than Christlike fashion. Confession is a time of cleansing and of accepting God's forgiveness. Only then can He fill me with His presence anew.

Another unloading of my concerns occurs when I pray for

wisdom in solving certain problems or intercede for others with enormous needs. Prayer truly is a way of taking the problems to the Master. Leaving the concerns with Him frees my mind for Him to speak to me.

Bible study.—A storehouse of biblical knowledge is necessary before we can pray *in the will of God*. So much of God's will is already spelled out for us in our Christian guidebook, the Bible. We need to know His laws and principles so we won't pray amiss.

A foolish, misguided woman once told me about a man with whom she was infatuated. They worked in the same firm. He was married. So was she. She indicated that she was praying for the man to become as attracted to her as she was to him. Rather piously she added, "but only, of course, if it is God's will."

She seemed surprised to hear that God had already spoken on that matter. The answer was, and remains, a big no.

Occasionally we hear someone praying for lost friends or family members. After pleading for their salvation, they then add, "if it is Your will."

Again, God has already shared His will and desire that all might be saved. Thus when we pray for those who've never accepted Christ as Savior, we know that we're praying within God's will. Our mind is in tune with His Spirit.

We don't have such clear directions for all of our praying, of course, but we can experience the power of prayer more fully when it is possible to pray within God's will. At other times we must pray, "Thy will be done."

Once into Bible study several guidelines help me.

• *Take time to mull over a verse or section of Scripture.*—Explore possible aspects of a verse even while praying that God will reveal the lesson He wants to give us on that particular day, with that particular verse or verses.

A "for instance" is the story of the woman at the well (see John 4). Note verse 28 informs us that she left her water jar and went to tell.

One day I stopped at that verse. (If we ask the Lord to

throw up a stop sign when we reach a teachable spot, He will.) I mused, *Why is that mundane little event mentioned?*

• *Write down thoughts which come.*—Picking up my note-book and pen, I jotted down possible answers. Her spiritual revelation was so overwhelming that she forgot why she went to the well. Physical water was no longer a top priority. She couldn't wait to tell people what she had learned, a water pot would be an unnecessary encumbrance. Those at the well might be thirsty and could use it.

Thoughts tumbled around like children in a play area filled with plastic balls.

• *Note today how the verses apply personally.*—My notes continued: What about you, Fayly? Do you still get so excited over telling people about Jesus that mundane, everyday tasks are easily dropped or forgotten? Have you lost your first zeal? Have your priorities become scrambled?

• *Consider attitude.*—A proper state of mind is vital to effective Bible study. A planned expectation helps.

One of my husband's majors was geology. Rock hound expeditions were fun times (and inexpensive) when our children were young.

One Saturday we headed for an area listed as a great place to find fire agates. Arriving at the general location given on our map, we donned our day packs and headed toward the hills. We expected to find the shimmering stones. And we did! Everytime one of us would spot an agate it would be accompanied with a squeal of excitement.

Bible study is that way if we expect it to be so. We can anticipate the "ah ha" moment—the time when God reveals another truth tailor-made for us on that particular day.

Meditation.—Though God's primary way of sharing His thoughts with us is through the Bible, He speaks to us by impressions. Meditation gives us opportunity to equalize outside pressures which push against us with strengthened inner spiritual force. Without the equalization of those forces, we're apt to be crushed by the stress of living in today's world.

Taking several brief meditation breaks throughout the day

gives us opportunity to ask, "God, what do You want to say to me? How would You deal with this situation? Fill me with Your peace. Give me Your wise direction for decision making."

Meditation times can be as brief as a moment at a desk. Closed eyes do help shut out distractions. It's easier to focus on the Master.

If schedules and circumstances permit, a 10- or 15-minute time-out away from people is refreshing, relaxing, and rewarding. Find a comfortable spot and do some gentle neck- and muscle-relaxing exercises. Then focus your mind on the Savior.

Once you make the time to be with God and develop techniques which help you focus, you will experience accelerated spiritual growth. Sermons and Bible classes at church or on TV and radio will still provide insights which aid growth. Yet your time alone with God will provide special enrichment.

Maintain top priority.—Most of us agree that prayer, Bible study, and meditation time are essential for spiritual growth. Now how do we work that into our crammed schedules?

We start with actually writing it on our calendar of activities. The mere act of scheduling it reminds us that it is top priority. Some days may be so hectic that only 10 or 15 minutes are possible. Yet without scheduled time we probably wouldn't even spend that much time in study.

Various phases of life and circumstances affect our schedules so we must constantly reassess and make adjustments. We'll find that when we crave that time with the Lord, we'll manage.

Interestingly enough, when we make time for quality time with God, we accomplish more in the time which is left. It's like tithing. Ninety percent has greater buying power than 100 percent, when 10 percent of God's money is given back to Him.

Share in Fellowship

We've talked about some of the ways we learn things God wants us to know. Another important conduit He uses is fellowship with other Christians.

I like the story of the child who wanted to sleep with his parents because he was scared. His mother told him there was no need to be afraid because God was with him.

To which the child responded, "But I want someone with skin on."

Sometimes we want advice and encouragement from someone with skin. God has provided that through some of His other children.

I can share my innermost thoughts with several dear, precious women. I don't have to fear that they won't understand or that they'll think less of me if I expose my human weaknesses. They pray with me and for me. They're my most important support group outside of my husband, children, and parents. They are friends, prayermates, and encouragers. Often one will say something which reinforces or affirms some lesson God is teaching me at the time.

Most of us need some special confidants in our lives. We need to trust enough to share. I confess that in my younger years I was afraid to bare my soul for fear someone might think I wasn't as good a Christian as I should be.

From my vantage point now I realize how foolish and prideful I was then. Only after finally admitting my humanity could God use friends to help me.

In the Bible are many instances where God asked people to search themselves and admit their needs. Only then could He deal with them. When we practice openness with others, it's so much easier to be open and honest with God.

If you have a helpful support base of Christian friends and family, you understand. If you don't, you need to start developing one.

Minister Within Your Giftedness

Growing spiritually also involves ministry. If we are trying to follow Jesus' way, we'll help others. When we use our special gifts, we will experience *joy* in ministry.

During my "Miz Piggy" stage I tried to minister in ways

which weren't suited to my gifts. In attempting to use other gifts, I sometimes deprived those possessing the gifts the joy of service. And I felt like a miserable failure because I tried to do things outside the realm of my giftedness. I missed the joy!

Discover your gifts.—As you discover and use your gifts, you will experience the joy of fulfilling ministry. Chapter 5 has help for you.

Balance faith with works.—Is it possible to spend so much time ministering that we don't have time for renewal? Yes. It is probably our greatest area of tension. Balancing faith with works requires constant vigilance and discipline. Ministering within the scope of our own gifts helps us say no to some ministry opportunities and needs. Finding the proper balance is not easy, yet it can be done. Prayer and meditation periods give us opportunities for assessment. Then with God's guidance we can come closer to the happy balance.

Maintain a Teachable Mode

A 91-year-old woman is still taking courses at Grand Canyon University. Another friend, whose children are now grown, is taking Greek and Hebrew. She always wished she could study the Bible in the original languages. Another friend is doing home study on her 69th book in the Church Study Course program. Wouldn't you agree that these women have programmed themselves into the teachable mode?

These days there are so many exciting ways to continue growing. Conferences and workshops are practical. Not only is the subject matter relevant, but the inspiration of being with others who have similar interests, concerns, and experiences is encouraging and fun!

Several years ago while leading wives during a National Deacons Conference at Glorieta Baptist Conference Center, I met a "flock" of young adults from another state. Young deacons and their wives had taken vacation time to attend the conference. Ten of them had traveled together in a van. They had so much fun together that their Christian joy was contagious.

In that same conference was a retired bivocational church planter and his wife who had brought a young deacon and his wife. They wanted the younger couple to catch the excitement which comes from continued study and growth.

An older couple was also there. The husband had been a deacon for many years. At one of the breaks I suggested that probably both of them could be teaching during the week. They laughed demurely. Then the husband said, "We keep coming because we always learn new things." His wife added, "And we like the mind stretching which comes from learning. It's stimulating!"

In addition to deacons and wives conferences at Ridgecrest and Glorieta Baptist Conference Centers, most state conventions provide training opportunities. Associations and individual churches often schedule similar events.

Many deacons and wives have gone through the Master-Life study. Not only does it prepare you for quality Christian living, but those who complete it feel they are better qualified for ministry and leadership.

Deacons' wives of this era have books and learning resources available. Whether used for personal study or in groups, materials and products can assist in ongoing spiritual development. The book, *Priorities in Ministry* by Ernest Mosely,[2] is one which you and your husband will find helpful. Discussion of his suggested priorities can help you and your husband as you work out your own priorities in ministry.

Undoubtedly your husband has a copy of *The Ministry of Baptist Deacons* by Robert Sheffield.[3] You will find the chapters dealing with caregivers and growing in ministry effectiveness particularly helpful as you support and work with your husband.

The quarterly magazine, *The Deacon*,[4] includes articles for wives. As a vital part of deacon ministry, you will find current ideas and inspiration.

One gauge of our continuing spiritual growth is that assessment mirror. If each of us can still look at ourselves and say, "Oh, I'm still growing up, I'm still learning," then we'll know we are doing our part so God can do His.

[1]From the *Revised Standard Version of the Bible*, copyrighted 1946, 1952, ©
1971,1973.
[2]Ernest E. Mosely, *Priorities in Ministry* (Nashville: Convention Press, 1978).
[3]Robert Sheffield, *The Ministry of Baptist Deacons*, (Nashville: Convention
Press, 1990).
[4]*The Deacon* is available on the Dated Literature Order Form or by calling
1-800-458-2772.

*Fayly H. Cothern is a retired minister's wife, an experienced free-lance
writer, and a conference leader who lives in Phoenix, Arizona.*

Chapter 4

Little House on the Highway

Denise George

Above her kitchen sink, Sandy keeps a little green plaque that says: "Eat a Live Bullfrog the First Thing Each Morning . . . That Will Be the Worst Thing You'll Have to Do All Day!"

It works. No, Sandy doesn't eat a live bullfrog each morning, but the plaque makes her smile as she faces the sink full of breakfast dishes; the scattered breakfast granola; two active children rushing out the backdoor to school; and her list of appointments, meetings, luncheons, and carpooling treks for the day.

As a busy deacon's wife, Sandy often feels like a bullfrog.

"Sometimes I feel like a bullfrog sitting in the middle of a highway during five o'clock traffic . . . with a hopper broken!" she laughs.

And she's not alone.

Life in the Fast Lane

I love the "Proverbs 31 woman." She has been an inspiration to me since my girlhood.

But, as hard as she worked, as busy as her days, I believe she would have a hard time keeping up with today's deacon's wife!

True, the wife in Proverbs 31:10 got up early and went to bed late, worked outside the home, cooked, sewed, ministered to the poor and needy, took care of her children, and supported her husband in his role. On some days, no doubt, she, too, felt like a bullfrog. But there's a difference.

She had "servant girls." Notice that "girl" is plural—girls. In fact, I believe she had a whole house of servant girls to help her with her many responsibilities. Yes, I know she didn't have push-button gadgets such as dishwashers, washing machines, microwave ovens, vacuum cleaners, and all those conveniences that are supposed to help us and save us loads of time. But, think on this: She also didn't have gadget-repair people tromping through the house during supper time to fix those modern conveniences. And she never had a flat tire or dead car battery on her way to the Ladies Auxiliary luncheon where she had to give the opening prayer. And she never had the electricity pop off while she had a prepackaged lasagna in the oven, an automatic bread-making machine on bake, and a cake being microwaved. I have a feeling her husband never once in all their marriage told her: "Honey, I've got to be in Chicago for a luncheon meeting; and if the plane's on time, I'll be home for our dinner party. But if it's late, would you please entertain the Smiths and the Harrisons and serve the soup? I'll get home as soon as I can."

Let's face it. High technology makes for high-tech stress.

Dealing with Everyday Stress

Stress can cripple the best marriage. But I've found that it's not the disasters of life that injure spouse and family relationships. When a loved one dies or we face major surgery or one of the kids break a leg, somehow we manage. Usually, during our times of greatest crisis, throngs of people come to our backdoor with heaping bowls of instant banana pudding or microwavable chicken casseroles. The good people from the church often jump in with both feet and help us get back on our feet. Candlelight dinners and husband-wife romance might be put on hold for a while. Communication with each other might be spotty. But, all in all, the relationship suffers little. Often, in fact, a marriage is strengthened by a crisis and a general pulling together to get through it.

But, there's another kind of high-tech stress that can seriously hurt a marriage. It goes something like this:

You've had a hard day at work. The kids are next door playing softball, and you breathe a prayer of thanksgiving for a moment of quiet. You kick off your shoes, plop down in your favorite chair, switch on the news, pick up the new issue of *Royal Service,* and call the pizza delivery service to bring supper.

That's when your husband walks in the front door with the entire finance committee.

"Honey," he announces, "I'd like for you to meet Frank and Jim and Barney. They've just come on the finance committee. By the way, we're starved. I hope you've planned a special dinner!"

Later that night, after the finance committee has devoured six pepperoni pizzas, the rest of the leftover tuna casserole, and a whole bag of spinach-colored pasta, pillow talk may sound something like this.

Husband: "I distinctly remember telling you that the finance committee was coming for dinner tonight! You just weren't listening!"

Wife: "You just *think* you told me they were coming for dinner! You *never* said a word to me about it!"

Tears. More tears. The next day each one buys a big calendar with the words *Family Communicator* at the top and tapes it to the front of the refrigerator.

Watch Out for the "Little Things"

Research suggests that in today's world, one is as likely to be "nibbled to death" by everyday stresses as overwhelmed by tragedies. Those little irritating, everyday stresses can cause us to argue more with family members. They can cause in-laws to seem like outlaws. Family members caught in a cycle of everyday stress will become less happy about life, less efficient in jobs and schoolwork, and will slowly begin to withdraw from people. Everyday stress can even take a toll on your family's health.

The little everyday aggravations wear us down. It's those days when we have too much to do, too many directions to run, and not enough time to accomplish one third of what's written on our 20-item list.

It's the "little house on the highway syndrome," and it describes well the fast-lane life-style of many deacons' families today.

Listen to one wife describe a typical Monday morning in a deacon's household:

7:30 a.m. You, your deacon spouse, and your 2.5 children rush out the backdoor, late for work, late for school, late for a Baptist Women's meeting. As usual, you can't find your car keys. Breakfast? You hand a partially toasted, partially frozen prewaffled waffle to each kid.

"But, Mommy, my waffle's still frozen."

"Eat it!"

You find your keys, lock the backdoor, and then your son Johnny suddenly remembers he needs a clown costume for the school play—that day. You quickly pull a tube of lipstick from your purse, draw Bozo on his face, and hand him an umbrella.

Then daughter Cindy starts to scream. She left her math sheet on the kitchen table. You run in to retrieve it, and the telephone rings. It's Mrs. Murphy. She wants you to sing in the quartet at the church women's retreat next weekend. You tell her you sing like a crow. She laughs. She thinks you're kidding. You're not kidding. (Who would kid at 7:30 Monday morning?) You agree to sing, cackle, whistle—anything to get unleashed from the phone.

Outside, Bozo is playing with the car horn and poking Cindy with the umbrella. You close the garage door and buckle your bodies into the van. That's when you notice Cindy's shoes. They don't match. One foot's ready for church, the other for the tennis court.

And so goes the morning—a typical morning. After a day and evening of soccer practice, piano lessons, outreach supper, choir practice, business meeting, and 223 telephone calls, you collapse into bed exhausted. You go to sleep wondering what tomorrow will bring.

Making Bread

Not long ago, during a particularly grueling month's bout of little irritations, I decided to do what the Proverbs 31 woman would probably do if she was "stressed out"—make bread. There's a special stress-relieving quality about making bread. You can hit, box, and punch that glob of hard elastic dough until your frustration melts away. And you can call it kneading. Depending on how long it took to relieve the day's stresses is how long I kneaded that bread dough.

I made a lot of homemade bread around the clock for a whole month. I even got creative with it. I made orange bread, coconut bread, pineapple bread, lemon-peel bread, butterscotch bread, oatmeal bread—you get the picture. For breakfast I smeared the bread with cream cheese. For lunch I squirted it with pizza sauce. For supper I smothered it with turkey and gravy.

At first, my husband and kids were delighted. They could smell the home-baked aroma coming out the backdoor when they burst in from school and work. But, by the end of that month, they were weary of the stuff.

This fact dawned on me when my son, Christian, bounced in from school, took a deep breath, made a disgusting face, and exclaimed: "Oh no, Mom! P-l-e-a-s-e not homemade chocolate chip bread again!"

But that didn't stop me.

I can just imagine one day that Christian, when a grown man, will drive by a neighborhood bakery or walk by a restaurant and get a whiff of delicious homemade bread. He'll, no doubt, stop and remember, and probably say something like: "Yuk! That smells just like my mother's kitchen!"

The "C" Word

Did you ever wonder when the Proverbs 31 woman and her husband sat down and talked? Between the buying and planting and sewing and selling, I can imagine eyeball-to-eyeball, spouse-to-spouse communication may have been somewhat limited.

We hear a lot about communication these days, too much. I'm almost tired of being told how to learn to communicate. Just what is communication anyway? Webster's dictionary gives this definition: "To transmit information, thought, or feeling so that it is satisfactorily received or understood."

That's simple enough, so why all the fuss?

Even though time was limited in the Proverbs 31 woman's busy schedule, one thing's for sure: Her husband certainly knew how to communicate!

"Her husband also praises her. He says, 'There are many excellent wives, but you are better than all of them' " (Prov. 31:28-29, NCV).[1]

One well-worded message like that from a husband communicates! That kind of communication will last a long time. It's short and sweet, but full of tenderness, love, and appreciation—and truth!

In the closing verses of Proverbs, its writer, King Solomon, told husbands for the next several thousand years to communicate to their wives like this husband did. "Charm can fool you," he wrote, "and beauty can trick you. But a woman who respects the Lord should be praised. Give her the reward she has earned. She should be openly praised for what she has done" (Prov. 31:30-31, NCV). Amen!

Communication shouldn't be an unpleasant task. You don't have to sit in a ladder-back chair and stare at and talk to each other for hours each day. We shouldn't have to be told to communicate with our spouse! It is a natural act; and, whether or not we notice it, we communicate in various ways most of the time.

When my son giggles during Sunday morning church worship and I give him "the look," he quickly and genuinely receives and understands the information, thought, and feeling I have transmitted.

When my husband Timothy comes home from work and smoke is pouring from the oven and the kids are fighting and I've got tears on my cheeks and ear plugs in my ears, he doesn't need to ask me if I'm having a hard day. It communicates.

Some of the most potent communication comes from language that needs no words.

And, some of the sweetest communication comes from wordless "talk." A smile at the right time, an unexpected kiss on the cheek, an extra blanket thrown over cold feet, a surprise tank of gas and car wash, a nod of appreciation, a loving look across the breakfast table, a rose-remembered anniversary, a compliment about my homemade bread—nonverbal communication often speaks louder than words.

Communication happens all the time. In fact, a deliberate lack of communication can be the most deafening type of communication. Through glares, stares, knitted eyebrows, and zipped lips, entire volumes can be spoken between angry spouses who "aren't speaking to each other."

Perhaps our goal as husband and wife should not be to start communicating with each other, since we actually communicate all the time whether or not we know. Perhaps our goal should be to learn to communicate the way wise King Solomon suggested—with kind and loving words of genuine appreciation and praise. It doesn't take much time to give a nice compliment or throw a kiss or toss a wink. Yet these are the things of which good marriages are made. Even on our busiest days when we are literally running in opposite directions, the "two ships that pass in the kitchen" days, we can smile at each other as we sail by.

That's communication—at its best.

And What About Keeping Romance Alive?

I will admit to you—I married a bookworm. Timothy reads all the time. In fact, we spent our honeymoon at the Atlanta Discount Religious Bookstore! Timothy bought 35 books and refused to leave them in the car. There I was, a brand new bride with my brand new husband in a beautiful motel room on our wedding night with all of Calvin's commentaries!

At times during our marriage, I have had to be downright creative to get Timothy's attention. It's tough to compete with Calvin, Luther, Zwingli, and the Protestant Reformation!

I remember once reading a popular best-seller about how to get your husband's romantic attention. The author suggested that the wife wrap herself in Saran Wrap—only Saran Wrap—and greet her husband at the front door that evening!

No doubt, Saran Wrap sales skyrocketed!

I don't recommend this drastic action for a deacon's wife,

however. Just consider the possibilities. What if the person who rings your doorbell isn't your husband, but the television repair man, the mail carrier, the chairman of the deacons, the pastor, (or even worse) the pastor's wife?

I'd love to be a fly on the wall as you stand at the door "wrapped" trying to explain your unusual afternoon attire. No doubt, someone would request prayer for you (and your husband) at Wednesday night prayer meeting!

Now don't misunderstand me. Sometimes a new lacy night-gown can add a spark to romance, but I can tell you something about romance that is far more lasting. Holding hands, sitting by a glowing fire, silently reading a book together, eating a quiet supper, listening to music, watching a summer afternoon rain-storm—these are the things of which romance is made.

When Timothy calls me from the office in the afternoon just to say "hi," when he takes the kids out for pizza so I can grab a nap, when he deposits his dirty clothes directly into the wash-ing machine instead of the basket, when he buys me a paper-back book because he knows I'd love to read it, he doesn't real-ize it, but I see all these wonderful surprises as romantic.

The simple things, the quiet things, are the most meaningful to me. True romance is the enjoyment of just being together, the excitement of sharing a future, the goal of working hard togeth-er and overcoming obstacles, and the commitment to a quality life with each other. To think of romance as only a sexual experi-ence disregards a huge part of what romance really means.

Should We Schedule a "Date"?

I don't advocate making a weekly "date" with each other or scheduling an appointment to spend time together. This seems too artificial.

Meaningful communication with someone you love happens most often spontaneously. It is somewhat like prayer. The analo-gy would break down quickly if pushed, but consider this: If you truly love the Lord and are committed to Him, you'll think about Him, you'll speak to Him, you'll look up and smile at Him, and you'll want to spend time with Him—spontaneously all during your day and night. Yes, you might schedule certain devotional and prayer times (I enjoy my early morning "appointment" with the Lord each day), but some of the most meaningful times of communion will happen when you least expect it. Walking through a rose garden, watching a golden sunset, hearing a child's happy laughter, or reading a letter from a longtime friend can inspire within you a moment of prayer with the Father that could never be penciled in on your calendar.

There are lots of ways to say "I love you" in prayer and in marriage. And not one of them requires an appointment book or Saran Wrap!

Deacon Family Facts

Why is time so limited in the deacon's family? Why do deacon couples experience a great amount of stress? Why is the family calendar so crowded?

I don't have to tell you that being married to a deacon isn't easy. As a deacon, your husband has enormous responsibilities not only in his employment but also in his church. A paid church staff worker can devote full time to ministry; a deacon, however, must make time for both secular employment *and* ministry. And ministry punches no time clock! Ministry is like motherhood—it never ends. It involves around-the-clock commitment. There's always something to do when one is involved in ministry because someone always has a need, usually an unexpected urgent need at the most inappropriate and inconvenient times.

The expectations that greet a deacon couple are unlike those that greet the average church member. A deacon and his wife stand as a pillar of the church. Much is expected of them; much is entrusted to them.

You and your husband have been "set aside" for a special function in the body of Christ—the church. Your mutual job is an important one. Thus, church services and church meetings will probably eat up much of the "free time" you once enjoyed as a couple. Being a primary support to the pastor can bring unplanned and unexpected needs and time away from family.

You, as a deacon's wife, may be more readily called on to chair a committee, teach a class, serve as Sunday School director, or speak at a social function because of your unique position. This can be especially time and energy draining if you work a full-time job outside the home or manage a household alone or have children or elderly parents to care for. You'll know time and stress demands that most worshipers in the pew on Sunday mornings will never experience or even know about.

A deacon's family is considered a Christian model of home and marriage by others in the church family. Parents in the congregation will watch the deacon's family to learn good parenting skills. Young women in the church will look to the deacon's wife to learn how to be a Christian woman in their personal spiritual lives, in their future homes, churches, and communities. It's a big responsibility to be an example for others to follow.

But Consider the Bonuses

Even though you must deal with time and energy demands, just think of the opportunities given you as a deacon's wife! Unlike other women in the church, you have an automatically opened door to ministry. You can move into different areas of ministry easily and use your God-given gifts where you feel most needed. Because of your family's position in the church, you'll be kept informed about illnesses, deaths, births, marriages, and all that happens within the congregational family. Working together with other deacon couples and officers in the church to meet needs and solve problems will bring you close friendships that you might not otherwise develop.

Why Must the Marriage Be Strong?

Because of the gift of ministry you and your husband have been given, you must work hard to keep your marriage strong. Why? I can think of four good reasons. No doubt you can think of many more.

A solid marriage provides a secure base on which the family can minister and serve others.—Precious time and energy are not squandered in marital bickering and immature behavior when the marriage foundation is strong. If you can be known to have your home life and marriage under control, then you'll speak volumes to others in the church and community about God's values and priorities in life.

A stable marriage enables a deacon and his wife to communicate marriage and parenting skills to those in the church who need help with their own marriage and parenting skills.—How we need Christian couples to model marriages based on a commitment to God and to each other!

When their marriage is good, a deacon couple can be free to reach out to others in the church family who need them.—It's hard to help others with their problems when we are tied up with our own.

A loving marriage allows each partner to use his or her God-given gifts to full potential.—Neither partner is threatened by, or jealous of, the good gifts of the other. The husband and wife can genuinely complement, encourage, and support each other in active and productive ministry. Everyone benefits—the wife, the husband, the children, the church. Each is free to be guided by the leadership of the Holy Spirit to use his or her gifts to the glory of the Lord.

When Conflict Rears Its Ugly Head

No matter how good and loving and solid and stable a marriage, there will be times when couples will experience conflict within the family nest. No two birds can build a home together, share it, repair it, clean it, and raise demanding little birds and always agree on everything. We're not talking about *Family Feud*, but from time to time all spouses will disagree. Take it from me, it's a fact. The union of marriage presents a smorgasbord of potential conflicts.

What do deacon couples disagree and argue about? They disagree about money, in-laws, child discipline, calendars, vacation spots, sex, politics, religion, who takes out the trash, and all the things other couples might fuss over.

What can we do about conflict in our marriage? I have several suggestions that have worked for us.

Choose your battles.—It doesn't really matter how many an-
gels can be squeezed onto the head of a pin. But it does matter
if one partner wants to tithe and give to missions and the other
doesn't. It doesn't really matter if deacons meeting runs an hour
too long and the candlelight dinner is put on hold. But it does
matter if the family's summer vacation is rescheduled four
times because other deacons in the church aren't pulling their
own weight.

Before you initiate a "discussion" over an issue, look the
issue square in the face. Ask three questions: So what? Who
cares? and What does it matter in light of eternity?

Then overlook the small things that don't really matter.
Choose not to deal with potential little skirmishes that have no
lasting value. Save your energy for the things that do matter.
Blow your bugle for those times that call for battle, for those important issues that have eternal consequences.

Learn how to disagree agreeably.—"You fat, unappreciative
pig" is no way to begin a discussion. Neither is throwing a chair
at your spouse.

King Solomon penned these famous words: "Stirring milk
makes butter. Twisting noses makes them bleed. And stirring
up anger makes trouble" (Prov. 30:33, NCV).

If you want to wave a red flag in front of a snorting bull and
really "stir up anger," just throw something at your husband!

I had a friend who hurled a television at her husband because he refused to go with her to the church marriage enrichment seminar potluck supper. Throwing eye darts at him, she
stepped over the broken picture tube and left her husband
wondering who would win the World Series. Then she
slammed the den door, jerked on her coat, and took her pot of
baked beans to a nearby park, and, still fuming, ate every last
one of them. She drove home late that night still feeling like an
angry volcano (in more ways than one). Had she not become so
sick, she might still be angry with her husband!

I have three suggestions for "fighting fair" in marriage.

• Let your anger cool down before you even attempt a discussion, and then take turns and voice your protests gingerly.

• Hug each other before you begin the discussion, and hold hands the entire time you talk it out.

• Settle it quickly, forgive and forget, and pray together before you retire for the night. Then hug each other again. And if either of you has heard a funny joke that day, share it and laugh together.

Face the plain and simple facts of marriage.—The fact is that no matter how wonderful your spouse may be, no matter how much he loves you, no matter how many times he's been voted "who's who in the church," he is still a human being. And a human being cannot meet all the needs we have as a woman and a wife. When we lean too hard on our husbands to meet our needs, to love us unconditionally, to give us significance and value, to satisfy our inner longings and general loneliness, we will always be disappointed.

Only Jesus Christ can love us as we want to be loved. Only Jesus Christ can give our lives the significance and meaning we crave. Only Jesus Christ can fill our soul-hungry hearts. While no marriage partner is perfect, Jesus Christ *is* perfect.

Imagine the freedom each partner in marriage can experience when each is relieved of the tremendous pressure of trying to be all things to his or her spouse. Imagine the amount of ministry that can be accomplished by using the enormous amount of energy saved from trying to meet all of each other's needs.

When we can look squarely at our spouse with a realistic eye, know and love him for who he is and what God would have him to become, we gain a new perspective on this unique and difficult relationship called marriage. We accept him as he is, and, if he needs to be changed in some areas of his personality, we let the Lord handle it. We do the possible; we ask the Lord to do the impossible. We learn to ignore the minor irritations and pray hard over the major obstacles to the relationship. We learn to slip our feet into our husband's shoes and ask the Lord for understanding into his thoughts, his feelings, his actions. We learn to laugh when life gets too serious—those times when we wonder if we can tolerate another day with this imperfect human creation with whom we share our love, our bed, our home, our money, our children, and our lives. We learn to thank God deeply that the marriage has stayed together in a world that is quickly falling apart. And we learn to start seeing this God-given man-gift to us with God's eyes, hearing him with God's ears, and loving him with God's heart.

For that is marriage, the good and the bad, the better and the worst, the joy and the pain, the smiles and the frowns. I am convinced that marriage can only work when Jesus Christ is securely stationed in the home and in the hearts of husbands and wives who commit themselves to the Lord and to each other. Marriage at its best is one where a woman and man respect the Lord.

And if being married to a deacon sometimes makes us feel like bullfrogs with broken hoppers sitting in the middle of a highway during 5:00 traffic, well we can take that to the Lord, too!

[1]From *The Everyday Bible*, New Century Version, copyright 1991 by Word Publishing, Dallas, Texas. Used by permission. Subsequent quotations are marked NCV.

Denise George is the author of nine books, including Becoming Tender in a Tough World *(Broadman Press) and* Healing for Wounded Women *(Broadman Press). She has sold more than five hundred feature articles to numerous publications including* Redbook, Guideposts, Essence, Decision, Catholic Digest, The Christian Reader, Home Life, Lutheran Digest, *and many others. Denise lives in Birmingham, Alabama.*

Chapter 5

A Cup of Cold Water

Barbara Sheffield

A thirsty person can receive a cool drink from a water fountain. But the joy of ministry is found in offering the cup of cold water. The thirst is quenched, but the one who reaches out with the cup often receives the greater blessing.

There was a time when I went once a month to visit residents in a local nursing home. To be perfectly honest, I didn't look forward to this. I dreaded seeing the people in various stages of declining health. I felt sorry for them, but I didn't think there was anything I could do to make their lives better. I was expected to go, so I went. After the small group of us visited with the residents, we sang hymns. Many of the men and women tried to sing along with us, and others tapped a foot or hand in the rhythm of the songs. Frequently tears trickled down a cheek as they remembered past times when they, too, could join in singing praises to our Lord. As I looked into the faces of those precious people, I soon forgot that I was there to minister to them. The excitement and joy in their faces ministered to me! I always left that place with a smile and a happy heart.

All of us minister most effectively when we allow ourselves to be used within the sphere of our own unique personalities and gifts. We all have different experiences, emotions, and personal goals. The New Testament shows us that each Christian has received a special gift to be used in caring for one another. No two of us are alike. We must spend time getting to know which gifts the Holy Spirit has given us. What do we enjoy doing? What gifts have others recognized in us? What gifts do others call on us to use?

We need to be willing to serve, but we should also know our physical and emotional limitations. Realize that we can't do it all. We should not say yes to every job we are asked to do. Perhaps we should consider changing the responsibilities of the nominating committee to "gift search" committee.[1] Sometimes we know that a ministry opportunity is not within our gifted area. Yet we feel guilty if there is a vacancy and no one is willing to fill it. During these times, we need to help someone with the appropriate gift to have the joy of service. This is not to say that our ministry will always be the same. As we grow spiritually and as our priorities and interests shift, our gifts can find expression in a variety of ways. Don't allow other people to decide your direction in ministry. Be yourself.

Meeting Needs

We each have special skills that can be used for ministry. Some of you are project people. You minister best through well-planned events. You can serve on committees and minister through structured activities. You may volunteer your time to help in the church office or at hospitals one day a week. You may lead a Bible study at a retirement or nursing home on Sunday afternoons or Thursday mornings. You can write notes and make telephone calls. You may visit homebound church members on a regular basis. You may serve along with your husband in preparation for the Lord's Supper observance and baptism.

Some of you can be more spontaneous in meeting needs. You see a need and meet it. In crises situations you are able to remain calm and manage details.

During the hospitalization of a church member, a deacon's wife provided transportation for his wife who did not drive. After parents brought home their newborn, the deacons wives provided dinner. One wife offered to stay with the baby so the new mom could get some much-needed rest. Some women take care of children after school or stay with an elderly parent so that the caregiver can wash her hair, do laundry, clean house, shop, or read.

Some of you find yourselves suited to outreach ministry. You contact visitors who have worshiped on Sunday. You share your faith with unchurched and unsaved and explain the mission of your church and denomination. You visit in homes and the hospital.

Others of you feel your gifts are better directed toward ministry to church members. You work through missions organizations to educate the congregation. You seek to help church members find ways of service in and through the church. You teach Sunday School classes and work with choirs and Discipleship Training groups. You help with children and youth during Vacation Bible School and January Bible Study.

Time Availability

Knowing our time availability for ministry is important. In these days when both husband and wife work outside the home, there seems to be little time left after the completion of chores. It is often difficult to find time to minister when young children need help with homework or a science project. Little League, GAs, RAs, Mission Friends, and Scouts compete for attention. As they grow, children can learn the importance of sharing and ministry. After children grow older and during the empty-nest years, ministry often takes a new direction.

Consider a time budget and make a priority list to maximize your time. Don't leave out your family. Make a schedule for each day including activities involving your children. If something cannot be done today, move it to tomorrow's list. Use spare minutes and don't waste time. While waiting for a doctor's appointment, make a grocery list or study your Sunday School lesson. Relax by reading a magazine or beginning a book you've not had time to read. Don't become a slave to schedules to the exclusion of time for yourself. Save time (make time) for exercise, recreation, and time with your husband. A break from the routine prevents each of us from becoming dull and occasionally bitter. Get up a few minutes earlier than normal and train your children to go to bed at a certain time so that you will have some time for yourself or with your husband. Exercise and take walks together through the neighborhood or even in a shopping mall. Ministry is most effective if we set aside time for relaxation and renewal.

Find easier ways of doing things. If you have trouble finding time to clean your entire house at one time, try dusting one day, vacuuming another, and cleaning the bathrooms another. Instead of doing laundry all day on Saturday, I put a load of clothes or towels in the washer on my way to work and transfer them to the dryer when I get home. I have time to fold them during the evening news. A quick stop at the grocery store on the way home from work for milk, bread, and bananas allows me to make a trip once a week or every other week for major items.

One of the most time-consuming activities in most families is meal preparation. Often I've found it as easy to double a recipe as it would be to make one casserole. I can serve one and freeze one for later or take it to someone. Line your casserole dish with foil, freeze, then remove the food from the dish. This leaves the dish free to be used while the food remains frozen. When ready to cook, unwrap it and put it back in the dish. It's almost as quick to brown three pounds of ground meat as it is to brown one pound. Use one and freeze the other meat for use at another time. If a recipe makes more than one loaf of bread, serve one and share or freeze the others. Make congealed and frozen salads ahead.

Keep items in your pantry that permit you to fix a quick meal on short notice. A box of macaroni and cheese becomes a special treat if you add a chopped tomato, pickle relish, and some chicken, ham, or tuna. Freeze leftover pot roast, chicken, and vegetables to use later as a starter for soup. I frequently boil a chicken, remove the meat from the bones, place it in a plastic container, and cover it with broth. After the broth cools, I remove any visible fat and freeze the chicken in broth for use at a later date. I freeze the rest of the broth in muffin tins and use it to season vegetables and other foods. Grate several pounds of cheese and freeze. Chop nuts and onions and freeze. Plan menus in advance and make a detailed grocery list. Serve buffet style from the kitchen counter.

Learn to delegate. You probably are not the only person in your family who can use a vacuum cleaner or dust cloth. Children can assume responsibility for folding and putting away their clothes and taking care of their own rooms. Relax your standards. What seems to be a clean room to your 10-year-old son may not seem clean to you, but it is clean enough. Learn to close the door to his room if necessary.

Ministering Relationships

We must earn the right to minister. We need to establish trusting relationships before we can have the freedom to minister. There are many ways to show that we care. We can visit in the supermarket. We can visit at church as we meet new members and renew relationships with those who sit across the sanctuary from us. As you worship in your church, sit in a different pew from time to time. Many times we overlook visitors and new church members because we aren't aware of their presence.

We can get to know families by rejoicing in good times such as a wedding, the birth of a new baby, school graduation, birthdays, anniversaries, or a new home. Then, we can minister in crises. Crises disrupt the normal routine of a family. We can step in with food and offers to run errands or make telephone calls to help ease stress. Often people hesitate to ask for help if we say, "If you need anything, let me know."

A pastor's wife shared her experience. When she and her husband arrived at their new church with their family, a deacon's wife made an offer to help. The pastor's wife, with a new baby, was frazzled trying to unpack the mountains of boxes in their new home. She decided to take the deacon's wife up on her offer. The deacon's wife was reluctant to come over but did. The baby cried all during her stay, and the young mother was unable to get much done. The whole situation was uncomfortable for the pastor's wife and the deacon's wife.

Try to be specific in helping manage details and be sure you are sincere. Never imply that your ministry is a chore or something done out of a sense of duty. Don't deliver a book or make a visit because you are expected to. Do it because you care.

Following a crisis, we tend to forget about the situation. Be involved in a follow-up ministry. Birthdays, anniversaries, and holidays are particularly difficult for families following the death of a spouse, a child, or friend. We don't recover from this type of loss in a few weeks. It usually takes months or years. A friend of my mother sent me flowers on my mother's birthday the year following her death. A deacon couple who have a big Fourth of July family gathering each year always include several people who would be alone on that day. On Thanksgiving Day another couple who live far from their own family adopt several people to share the meal with them.

In every church there are groups of people who share many things with one another. Within these groups a wonderful fellowship and friendship exists. Newcomers often find it difficult to get into these inner circles. Part of our ministry would be to help fellow Christians become a part of our family of faith. There are lonely people outside and inside our churches. Do your part in drawing new families into the warmth of your church. Make sure that they are aware of activities for their children and for the parents. Invite them for a cup of coffee at your home or at a local restaurant. Introduce them to your friends and to other people in the church who might have interests in common with them. Include them in fellowship groups. In times of crisis many people "slip through the crack" because we assume someone else is ministering. Quite often those overlooked are new or inactive members. It is not intentional on our part, but we often are not sensitive to needs.

My mother served as an example of helping others become part of the church. She had been a member of the same church for over 40 years and had many close friends there. When she moved with us to Nashville, Tennessee, we all wondered how she would adjust to her new life. After a few weeks, she asked me to take her to a retirement complex to visit some of the ladies she had met in her Sunday School class. She needed to develop new relationships, and she was willing to take the initiative. She spent many hours on the telephone visiting with her new friends. One of these was a lady who had been attending church for several years but had not moved her membership. Some time later during a Sunday morning worship service, Mother told me that she needed to sit on the end of the pew instead of her usual place. At the conclusion of the service, she walked with Mary Lou to the front of the church as this new friend united with the church on promise of her letter from another congregation.

Don't forget the families of your church staff. In every church my husband pastored, there were deacons and wives who adopted our kids. Sometimes grandparents whose own grandchildren lived in a distant city adopted our children. Frequently couples with teenagers needed to "borrow" our young children. Often friends kept our children, giving us some time to be alone.

We need to be available. Recently a friend told me she needed to talk to me. That is exactly what she needed. She didn't need me to talk to her. We met for about 30 minutes. When she left, she told me how much our "chat" had meant to her. After she left, I reminded myself that she needed to talk; I needed to listen with sensitivity. She needed my listening ear. She didn't need for me to give her advice or ask too many questions. Talking out the situation had enabled her to see some things in a new light and form some plans. I needed to pay attention to her and to remain impartial. I also needed to be calm and not to be shocked at things she told me. As she talked, I listened for more than facts. Her feelings were important. It was all right to have periods of silence. After this meeting, I followed up in a casual conversation. She had talked out her feelings and was able to move on.

Many times all we need to do is to listen. The ministry of our presence is important. We need to remember, however, that the "problem" belongs to someone else. Often we become so emotionally involved that we allow people to dump their problems on us. That's fine for them; the problem is now ours! We should be willing to listen and at times involve other people. But at all times we should keep confidences. Ask permission before including someone else.

Our caring ministry will not always take the same form. Ministry to young families may differ from ministry to singles and older adults. Ministry to young children and to adolescents may vary. *Caring for Folks from Birth to Death*[2] offers many helpful suggestions for ministry opportunities. *Equipping Deacons in Caring Skills*[3] and *Equipping Deacons in Caring Skills, Volume 2*[4] contain useful information about special needs ministries.

Let your ministry become a way of life.

Recipes

The following recipes are some you will find easy to put together quickly. Some freeze well and others make enough to serve and to share.

Cheese Soup[5]

6 cups diced potatoes
1 cup diced carrots
1 cup diced celery
1 cup diced onions
1 package of chopped broccoli
6 cubes chicken bouillon and 2 quarts water
(or 2 quarts of chicken stock)
2 cups of milk
1 cup sour cream
1 pound processed cheese, grated

Cook the first six ingredients until vegetables are tender. Add the last three ingredients. Simmer until thick. Freezes well.

Sausage Biscuits[6]

1 pound bulk sausage
3 cups buttermilk baking mix
8 oz. coarsely grated cheddar cheese
2 large eggs
$1/4$ cup milk
$1/2$ teaspoon salt
$1/8$ to $1/4$ teaspoon pepper
$1/4$ teaspoon dried thyme leaves
$1/8$ teaspoon ground ginger

In a large skillet cook sausage 6 to 8 minutes over moderate heat, breaking it up with a spoon, until meat is no longer pink and most of the fat has cooked out. Drain. Heat oven to 350 degrees. In a large bowl combine biscuit mix, cheese, and cooked sausage. In a small bowl beat eggs, milk, salt, pepper, thyme, and ginger. Add egg mixture to sausage mixture and mix well with hands. Shape mixture into 12 patties, about 3 inches in diameter and 1 inch thick, using about $1/3$ cup for each. Place 2 inches apart on an ungreased baking sheet. These biscuits freeze well. Pack in lunch boxes and they will be ready to eat at noon.

Raisin Bran Muffins

3 cups sugar
1 cup oil
4 eggs
1 quart buttermilk
5 cups all-purpose flour
5 teaspoons soda
2 teaspoons salt
1 teaspoon cloves
1 teaspoon nutmeg
1 teaspoon cinnamon
2 teaspoons vanilla flavoring
15 oz. Raisin Bran or Fruit & Fiber cereal

Combine ingredients in order. Can store in a tight container up to 4 weeks. Bake in muffin cups 15 minutes at 400 degrees.

Strawberry Walnut Bread

2 cups finely chopped walnuts
3 cups all-purpose flour
1 teaspoon baking soda
$1^1/2$ teaspoons cinnamon

$1/2$ teaspoon salt
$1/4$ teaspoon nutmeg
4 eggs, beaten
2 cups sugar
$1^1/2$ cups strawberries (fresh or frozen, thawed and chopped)
1 cup mashed bananas
1 cup cooking oil

Grease and flour two 9-by-5-by-3-inch loaf pans. Sprinkle $1/2$ cup nuts in the bottom of each pan. Stir together flour, soda, cinnamon, salt, and nutmeg. Combine remaining ingredients. Add to dry ingredients. Stir just until moistened. Stir in remaining nuts. Spoon batter into prepared pans. Bake 1 hour at 350 degrees.

Quickie Cheese Bread

1 egg, beaten
$1/2$ cup milk
$1^1/2$ cup baking mix
$3/4$ cup shredded cheese

Combine egg and milk. Add baking mix and $1/2$ cup cheese. Pour into greased 8-by-4-by-3-inch loaf pan. Top with remaining cheese. Bake 20 minutes at 400 degrees.

Brisket[7]

Place a 6-pound brisket in a long pan. Punch full of holes with knife. Sprinkle entire surface with:

    unseasoned meat tenderizer
    celery salt
    black pepper
    garlic salt
    seasoned salt

Work seasoning into meat. Mix $1/3$ cup Worcestershire sauce and $1/3$ cup liquid smoke. Pour over meat. Cover with foil and marinate overnight. Bake in 250 degree oven for 6 hours or until very tender. Cool and refrigerate overnight. Remove fat, strain juice, and slice meat. Cover meat with juice and reheat or freeze. (Keep one cooked and frozen, always prepared.)

Crescent-Pecan Chicken Casserole[8]

2 Tablespoons butter or margarine
$1/2$ cup chopped celery
$1/2$ cup chopped onion
3 cups cubed chicken breast, cooked
1 can cream of chicken soup
1 can cream of mushroom soup

1 8 oz. can water chestnuts, drained and sliced
1 4 oz. can sliced mushrooms, drained
$2/3$ cup mayonnaise
$1/2$ cup sour cream
$1/4$ teaspoon curry powder

Sauté celery and onions in butter. Add next 8 ingredients; heat but do not boil. Pour into a greased 9-by-13-inch baking dish.

Topping
1 can refrigerated Crescent dinner rolls
2-4 tablespoons melted margarine
$2/3$ cup shredded cheddar cheese
$1/2$ cup chopped pecans

Separate Crescent roll dough into 2 rectangles. Place over hot chicken mixture. Brush dough with melted butter. Sprinkle with cheese and pecans. Bake 20-25 minutes at 375 degrees until golden brown. (Can be made ahead and frozen; wait until ready to cook to add topping.)

Sausage and Rice Casserole
1 pound sausage (pork, beef, or turkey)
1 medium onion, chopped
1 clove garlic, chopped (optional)
1 cup chopped celery
$1/2$ cup chopped green sweet pepper
1 cup rice, uncooked
1 can cream of mushroom soup
2 cans cream of chicken soup

Brown meat with onion and garlic. Add celery and peppers. Simmer until tender. Drain. Add rice and soups. Stir. Bake in covered ungreased casserole 1 to $1^1/2$ hours at 325 degrees.

Shrimp Casserole
1 pound cooked, peeled shrimp
2 cans creamed soups
$1/2$ cup onion and green sweet peppers
1 cup rice, uncooked
$1/2$ stick melted margarine
1 can Rotel tomatoes

Mix ingredients. Baked in covered ungreased casserole 1 hour at 350 degrees.

Ground Beef Casserole

1 pound ground beef
1 medium onion, chopped
8 oz. frozen hash brown potatoes
1 can cream of mushroom or celery soup
2 cups sour cream
1 can onion rings

Brown and drain ground meat and onion. Add other ingredients and mix thoroughly. Pour into casserole and top with onion rings. Bake 30 minutes at 350 degrees.

Beef-Corn-Noodle Casserole

1 pound ground beef
1 medium onion, chopped
1 can whole kernel corn
1 can pimento, chopped
1 can cream of mushroom or cream of chicken soup
1 can cream of tomato soup
1 cup sour cream
1 6 oz. package noodles
salt and pepper to taste

Brown ground beef with onions. Cook noodles and drain. Combine all ingredients; bake in covered ungreased casserole 30-40 minutes at 350 degrees.

Beef Noodle Casserole

1 large package noodles
2 pounds ground beef, browned
1 medium onion, chopped and sauteed
2 large cans tomato sauce
1 tablespoons Worcestershire sauce
1 12-16 oz. carton creamed cottage cheese
1 cup sour cream
1 8 oz. package cream cheese
Parmesan cheese

Place cooked noodles in casserole dish. Stir together cottage cheese, sour cream, and cream cheese and put on top of noodles. Mix browned meat, onion, tomato sauce, and Worcestershire sauce. Pour on top of cheese mixture. Top with lots of Parmesan cheese. Bake 30-40 minutes at 350 degrees.

Chicken Rice Casserole

3 cups boiled chicken
1 medium onion, chopped
$1/2$ cup mayonnaise
$1/2$ cup chicken broth
1 package Uncle Ben's Wild Rice
1 can cream of celery soup
1 can sliced water chestnuts

Mix and bake covered for 45 minutes at 325 degrees.

Cream Chicken Casserole

1 box Escort crackers
1 stick margarine
2 cups diced chicken, cooked
8 oz. sour cream
2 cans creamed soups

Crush the crackers and blend with melted margarine. Put half on the bottom of a 9-by-13-inch dish. Mix chicken, sour cream, and creamed soups. Pour over the cracker mixture. Top with the remaining crackers and heat.

Corn Pudding

2 #2 cans creamed corn
6 eggs, beaten
$1/2$ cup flour
1 stick melted margarine
1 cup milk
4 tablespoons sugar (optional)
$1/2$ teaspoon salt

Mix well and pour into greased 2-quart casserole. Bake 1 hour at 350 degrees.

Rice

1 cup rice
$1/2$ stick margarine
2 cans beef or chicken broth
  (I usually use one of each)
1 medium onion, chopped

Melt margarine. Add other ingredients. Bake covered 45 minutes at 350 degrees.

Cranberry Salad

1 6 oz. package cherry jello
1 jar cranberry orange relish
1 16 oz. can crushed pineapple
  chopped nuts (optional)

Dissolve jello in $1^1/2$ cups hot water. Cool. Add relish, pineapple, and nuts. Congeal.

Cherry Delight

1 can Eagle Brand milk
9 oz. whipped topping, thawed
1 can cherry pie filling
1 tablespoon lemon juice
1 small can crushed pineapple
1 cup nuts (optional)
Blend and chill at least 4 hours.

Fruit Pizza

Spread one package of sugar cookie dough in a pizza pan. Bake 15 minutes. Mix 8 ounces cream cheese and 8 ounces whipped topping. Spread on cooled dough/crust. Add fruit of your choice on top or let each person "make their own."

Frozen Peanut Butter Pie

Blend $1^2/_3$ cups crushed chocolate wafers and 1 stick melted margarine for crust. Drizzle on chocolate syrup. Combine:

$2/_3$ cups peanut butter
1 cup milk
9 ounces whipped topping
8 ounces cream cheese
2 cups confectioners sugar
Pour into crust. Freeze. Drizzle chocolate syrup on top before serving.

[1] R. Wayne Jones, *Using Spiritual Gifts* (Nashville: Broadman Press, 1985), 15.

[2] James E. Hightower, Jr., *Caring for Folks from Birth to Death* (Nashville: Broadman Press, 1985).

[3] Homer D. Carter, *Equipping Deacons in Caring Skills* (Nashville: Convention Press, 1980).

[4] Robert L. Sheffield, *Equipping Deacons in Caring Skills, Volume 2* (Nashville: Convention Press, 1988).

[5] Mary E. Bess, *Tips for Ministers and Mates* (Nashville: Broadman Press, 1987), 88.

[6] Ibid., 95.

[7] Ibid., 91.

[8] Ibid., 90.

Barbara Sheffield is a middle-school teacher, free-lance writer, and conference leader for deacons' wives. She lives in Nashville, Tennessee.

Deacons can better serve your church with these helpful resources

The Deacon Magazine
This quarterly helps deacons understand and deal with key issues of ministry: conflict in the church, ministering in times of grief, visitation.

Equipping Deacons to Confront Conflict
Instructs both pastors and deacons on how to take positive action in times of church conflict. *(0-7673-1949-4; $7.95*)*

Deacons: Servant Models in the Church
Helps church members understand and deacons apply the biblically-based character qualities and ministry role of the deacon. Focuses on how deacons are partners with the pastor. *(0-8054-2463-6; $12.99*)*

Equipping Deacons in Caring Skills, Volume 1
Helps deacons improve caring skills, such as building trust, listening, determining needs, improving communication, finding solutions, referring, and follow-up. *(0-7673-2056-5; $10.95*)*

Deacons: Partners in Ministry and Growth Kit
Jim Henry, Senior Minister of First Baptist Church, Orlando, Florida, leads in this six-session training resource to teach deacons to become partners with your church staff in ministering to church members and visitors, and in promoting growth. *(0-7673-3896-0; $189.95*)*

Equipping Deacons in Caring Skills, Volume 2
Prepares deacons to recognize needs and provide practical care in crisis situations, such as abuse, divorce, unusual deaths, handicaps, financial stress, and others. *(0-7673-1943-5; $10.95*)*

Deacons: Growing in Commitment and Character Kit
This six-session video tape series is the perfect addition to your ongoing deacon ministry. With the use of humor, stories, and inspiration, Jim Henry leads deacons into a greater understanding of character and commitment. The series also contains several five-minute micro-messages that make great devotional inserts to any deacon conference or meeting. *(0-6330-2190-3; $199.95)*

Deacons as Leaders
Emphasizes the biblical leadership responsibility of the deacon—in times of church transition or working with pastors and staff. *(0-7673-1956-7; $5.00*)*

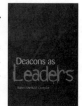